THE TIMOTHY INITIATIVE

Old Testament
Part Two

Greg Kappas and Jared Nelms, EDS.

Old Testament Part Two
Book Five in TTI's Foundational Curriculum

© 2012 by The Timothy Initiative

International Standard Book Number: 978-1477582756

All rights reserved. Published and Printed in the United States of America.

Library of Congress Cataloging-in-Publication Data

No part of this book covered by the copyrights heron may be reproduced or copied
in any form or by any means without written permission of the publisher.

Scripture quotations are from: The New King James Version
Copyright © 1979, 1980, 1982 by Thomas Nelson, Inc.
Used by permission. All rights reserved.

First Edition-North America
Second Edition

Acknowledgements

TTI gives special gratitude to the Docent Group and the leadership of Glenn Lucke and Jared Wilson (Docent Executive Editor for this project). The Docent writer, Steve Wamberg (Old Testament 1 and 2) demonstrated persistence on this project and we are thankful. TTI is very grateful for Rev. Jared Nelms and his extensive supplemental work on both Old Testament 1 and 2.

TTI also gives thanks to Dr. David Nelms, our Founder/President for his vision and influence to see this New Curriculum written. Dr. Nelms has lived humbly to see you succeed greatly in Jesus Christ.

We express our gratitude for the fine, long editorial labor to TTI Executive Editor and Director, Dr. Greg Kappas and the Executive Editorial Assistant and International Director, Rev. Jared Nelms. In addition we thank the entire TTI editorial team of Dr. David Nelms, Rev. Jesse Nelms, Rev. Larry Starkey, Rev. Lou Mancari and Dr. David Nichols. Each of you has given such remarkable grace to us and now to these church planters.

TTI is greatly appreciative of the Grace Fellowship elders, pastors, administrative staff, leaders and GF family. TTI was birthed out of this "church for all nations." Thank you for your generosity in launching this exponential network of church planting movements.

TTI's Board of Directors has given us freedom and focus to excel still more. We are deeply moved by these men and women of God. Our TTI investor base of financial and prayer partners extend around the globe. These individuals, churches, ministries, networks, corporations and organizations are essential and strategic to our collective health and Kingdom impact. Thank you!

We thank the TTI Continental Directors, Regional Directors, National Directors and District/Training Center Leaders for your ministry of love and commitment. You are the ones that forge into new and current frontiers with the Gospel. You truly are our heroes.

Finally, we are forever grateful to you, the church planter. You are planting an orchard, a church planting center through your local church that will touch your region and the world with the Gospel of Jesus Christ. We are honored to serve the Lord Jesus Christ and you. You will make a difference for our great God as you multiply healthy churches for His glory. We love you and believe in you!

TTI Staff Team
July 2010

THE TIMOTHY INITIATIVE

"What you have heard from me in the presence of many witnesses entrust to faithful men who will be able to teach others also."
2 Timothy 2:2

This workbook is the fifth of 10 workbooks which assist in equipping church planting leaders to start churches that saturate a region and help reach every man, woman and child with the Good News of our Lord. Below, is the list of this initial Curriculum.

TTI Curriculum

Workbook Number/Course:

1. Hermeneutics

2. Homiletics

3. Church Planting (New Testament – Acts, Evangelism, Discipleship, Spiritual Life, T4T)

4. Old Testament 1

5. **Old Testament 2**

6. New Testament Gospels

7. New Testament Pastoral Epistles

8. New Testament General Letters

9. Major Bible Doctrines

10. Apologetics-Church History-Spiritual Warfare

Table of Contents

Introduction 9

Chapter 1: The Creation Stage 10
(*Genesis 1-11*) Creation through 2165 BC

Chapter 2: The Patriarchal Stage 18
(*Genesis 12-50* and *Job*) 2165-1804 BC

Chapter 3: The Exodus Stage 28
(*Exodus, Leviticus, Numbers, Deuteronomy*) 1804-1405 BC

Chapter 4: The Conquest Stage 38
(*Joshua*) 1405-1390 BC

Chapter 5: The Judges Stage 42
(*Judges, Ruth, 1 Samuel 1-7*) 1390-1043 BC

Chapter 6: The United Kingdom Stage 48
(*1 Samuel 8-31, 2 Samuel, 1 Kings 1-11, 1 Chronicles, 2 Chronicles 1-9, Psalms, Proverbs, Ecclesiastes, Song of Solomon*) 1043-931 BC

Chapter 7: The Chaotic Kingdom Stage 63
(*1 Kings 12-22, 2 Kings 1-17, 2 Chronicles 10-36, Obadiah, Joel, Jonah, Amos, Hosea, Micah, Isaiah, Nahum, Zephaniah, Habakkuk, Jeremiah, Lamentations*) 931-605 BC

Chapter 8: The Captivity Stage 88
(*Ezekiel, Daniel*) 605-538 BC

Chapter 9: The Return Stage 98
(*Ezra, Esther, Nehemiah, Haggai, Zechariah, Malachi*) 548-400 BC

Endnotes 109

INTRODUCTION

Why Study the Old Testament in Its Historical Order?

Many courses that cover the books of the Bible, either Old or New Testament, use a survey approach. This means that each book studied in a course is often examined as a "book by itself." Every book is examined for:

1. Its key thought
2. Familiar verses
3. Its type of writing
4. Other identifying items that make the book stand out

But how do the books of the Bible fit together as God's great story of redemption? One way to answer this question is to place the books in historical (or "chronological") order, and watch the story unfold. That is the approach taken by Dr. H.L. Willmington in *Willmington's Guide to the Bible*.

Dr. Willmington's approach offers several answers to the question: "Why study the Old Testament in its historical order?" Some of those answers are:

- Studying the Old Testament in historical order helps us to understand *how the events from various books of the Old Testament fit together*. This will help the Church Planter teach the Bible with greater confidence.

- Studying the Old Testament in historical order lets us see *which Old Testament people lived at the same time*, together in history, even though they may appear in different Old Testament books.

- Studying the Old Testament in historical order often makes it easier *to relate the events of the Old Testament to ancient history recorded in sources other than the Old Testament*.

- Finally, studying the Old Testament in historical order helps us *gain understanding of the Old Testament as a connected whole instead of individual books*.

Dr. Willmington developed twelve main historical stages from Genesis through Revelation. He presented his work in an extended outline format much like the one you see in this book. *Willmington's Guide* has been of great value to tens of thousands of Bible students in schools and in homes since it was first published in 1981.

There are nine Old Testament stages in *Willmington's Guide* that take the reader from the beginnings of Genesis through the ministry of the prophet Malachi. This book follows Dr. Willmington's outline of those nine stages closely. The size and detail of Dr. Willmington's work has been reduced to better fit the needs of TTI Church Planters.

May you rejoice in God's Word through this study "as one who finds great treasure" (*Psa. 119:162*), in the Old Testament. God bless you as your understanding of the Scriptures grows!

NOTES

NOTES

CHAPTER ONE
THE CREATION STAGE

1. Creation Stage Overview[1]

A. The Creation Stage covers the time from the undated past to 2165 BC (*Genesis 1-11*).
- These dates are approximate due to differences in how ancient calendars were kept from culture to culture, and how family lines were recorded for history. Scholars have made great progress in accounting for these differences, but exact dates for events in ancient history are still difficult to determine.

B. The key people in the Creation Stage are Adam, Eve, Abel, Enoch and Noah.

C. The key events in the Creation Stage are: Creation, the Fall of Adam and Eve, the Flood of Noah, and the Tower of Babel.

D. The locations of the key events in this stage are:
- <u>The Creation</u>: the earth, then the Garden of Eden.
- <u>The Fall of Adam and Eve</u>: the Garden of Eden and the land just outside. This is probably near the source of the Tigris and Euphrates rivers in the highlands of modern Armenia.
- <u>The Flood</u>: the entire earth to Mesopotamia.
- <u>The Tower of Babel</u>: the plain of Shinar in ancient Babylonia in southern Mesopotamia.

E. There are several important "firsts" in this stage.
- The first created human, Adam (*Gen. 1:26*).
- The first human to be born, Cain (*Gen. 4:1*).
- The first marriage, between Adam and Eve (*Gen. 2:23-25*).
- The first murder, of Abel by Cain (*Gen. 4:8*).
- The first promise of the Messiah (*Gen. 3:15*, see *Rom. 16:20*).
- The beginnings of everything (*Gen. 1-2*).

2. The Bible Account of the Creation Stage

A. **Creation** (*Gen. 1-2*)
- History begins with God's creation of heaven and earth (*Gen. 1:1*).
  - ▶ The Hebrew word for "heaven" in *Gen. 1:1* is plural. The Bible says there are three heavens, all of which would have been created in the beginning.
    - ▷ The first heaven is the place for birds and clouds (see *Dan. 4:12, Mat. 6:26*).
    - ▷ The second heaven holds the sun, moon and stars (*Psa. 19:1*).
    - ▷ The third heaven is home to The Godhead, the angels and departed saints (*2 Cor. 12:2*).

- On the first day, God created light (*Gen. 1:2-5*).
  ▶ The Holy Spirit moved over the face of the waters.
  ▶ God divided the light from the darkness.
  ▶ God named the light "Day" and the darkness "Night."
- On the second day, God separated the waters above from the waters below with the firmament (*Gen. 1:6-8*).
  ▶ The waters above included rain and other kinds of precipitation.
  ▶ The waters below included river, seas, lakes, shallow and deep oceans and other land-based waters.
  ▶ The firmament is the span of sky or heaven that separates the waters above and the water below.
- On the third day, God gathered the waters below to make dry land appear and then created plant life (*Gen. 1:9-13*).
- On the fourth day, God created the sun, moon and stars as lights in the sky (*Gen. 1:14-19*).
  ▶ These lights divide the day from night. The sun rules the day, and the moon rules the night.
  ▶ These lights divide the seasons, days and years. They function much like a calendar.
  ▶ These lights are a constant reminder that creation is God's handiwork (see *Psa. 8:3* and *Rom. 1:19-20*).
- On the fifth day, God created sea creatures and birds (*Gen. 1:20-23*).
- On the sixth day, God created land creatures and man (*Gen. 1:24-31*).
  ▶ Only man is made in God's image (*Gen. 1:26*).
    ▷ *Psalm 8:5* reminds us that man is the highlight of God's creative work.
    ▷ In all creation, only man is truly designed for fellowship with God.
    ▷ Man was to exercise dominion over the natural world (*Gen. 1:27-28*).
    ▷ Man was free to enjoy all the trees of creation except the Tree of the Knowledge of Good and Evil (*Gen. 2:9, 16-17*).
    ▷ One of man's first assignments was to name the animals (*Gen. 2:19*).
    ▷ Man was given a wife. This marks the first marriage (*Gen. 2:18-25*).
  ▶ God describes Himself with the word "Us." This is the first evidence of the Trinity in the Bible (this concept is explained more in Book #9).
- On the seventh day, God rested (*Gen. 2:1-3*).
  ▶ This is the only place in the Bible where God is described as resting.

B. **The Fall of Adam and Eve into Sin** (*Gen. 3-5*)
- Satan spoke through the serpent in an attempt to break the fellowship between God and man (*Gen. 3:1*).
  ▶ The serpent cast doubt on God's Word.
- Eve added a lie to what God said (*Gen. 3:2-3*).
- The serpent denied God's Word (*Gen. 3:4-5*).
  ▶ The serpent lied and said Eve will not die if she eats the fruit.
  ▶ The serpent planted the half-truth that Eve will be like God if she eats the fruit.

NOTES

NOTES
- Adam and Eve chose to sin (*Gen. 3:6-7*).
  - They were tempted through the lust of the flesh, the lust of the eyes, and pride of life (see *1 Joh. 2:15-17*).
  - They attempted to hide their nakedness with fig leaves. This was an effort to make themselves "righteous" before God with their own efforts. They denied God's righteousness by doing so (see *Isa. 64:6*).
- Adam and Eve unsuccessfully tried to hide from God (*Gen. 3:8-13*).
  - Adam's attitude toward God changed from trust to fear.
  - Adam blamed Eve for his sin.
  - Eve blamed the serpent for her sin.

Questions:

What do you think would have been different if Adam and Eve had acknowledged their sin rather than try to blame others for their sin?

What is different when people today acknowledge their sin rather than blame someone else for it? (See *1 Joh. 1:8-10*).

- God judges the serpent, Adam and Eve (*Gen. 3:14-19*).
  - The serpent would eat dust and crawl on his belly.
  - The Seed of the woman would crush Satan's head.
  - Woman would suffer pain in childbirth.
  - Woman would be subject to man.
  - Man will have to work all his life.
  - The ground will be cursed and will produce thorns and weeds among the crops man must eat to live.
  - Man will die and decay.
- God shows grace as He deals with Adam and Eve.
  - God desired to bring Adam back into fellowship. He went after Adam (*Gen. 3:9*).
  - God promised a Savior (*Gen. 3:15*).
  - God provided clothing for Adam and Eve (*Gen. 3:21*).
  - God kept Adam and Eve away from the possibility of living forever in sin by blocking the way to the Tree of Life (*Gen. 3:22-24*).
    - If Adam and Eve had eaten from the Tree of Life, they would have lived forever. They had already shown that they could be tempted and fall to sin. Their ongoing sin could have multiplied into greater and greater evil. God's blocking the way to the Tree of Life was actually an act of mercy.
- God expelled Adam and Eve from the Garden of Eden (*Gen. 3:22-24*).
- Cain and Abel were Adam and Eve's first two sons mentioned in the Bi-

ble. They showed the difference between a person who was prepared to worship God and a person who did not approach God with a right heart (*Gen. 4*).

- ▶ Cain was a farmer who brought an offering of the fruit of the ground to God. God rejected Cain's offering because it was not from the heart as was Abel's (*Gen. 4:1-7*).[2]
- ▶ Abel was a shepherd who brought an offering to God of the best that he had: the firstborn of his flock. God accepted Abel's gift as more excellent than Cain's because of Abel's faith (see *Heb. 11:4*).
- ▶ God warned Cain that sin was waiting to attack him. He offered Cain the opportunity to change his attitude and "do well" (*Gen. 4:7*).
- ▶ Cain murdered Abel (*Gen. 4:8*).
  - ▷ Cain lied to God about murdering Abel (*Gen. 4:9*).
- ▶ God cursed Cain to be a fugitive, away from His blessings (Gen. 4:10-15).
  - ▷ It was a curse from the earth, which would no longer produce fruit for Cain's labor.
  - ▷ Cain showed no regret, but feared being murdered himself.
  - ▷ God marked Cain as a sign of His protection.
- ▶ Cain's family line is noted for their lack of honor towards God (Gen. 4:16-24). This did not mean every person in this family actively dishonored God, although many did. Rather, this means that Cain's family line was apathetic towards God.
  - ▷ They lived east of Eden in the land of Nod. "Nod" is a play on the word "vagabond" used in *verses 12* and *14*. <u>It signifies being distant from the presence of God.</u>
  - ▷ "Enoch" is the name of both Cain's firstborn son and the city Cain built and named after him. This son is <u>not</u> the righteous man of *Genesis 5*.
  - ▷ Lamech, Cain's great-great-great-grandson, was noted for several things that indicate his own defiance of God.
    - ◆ He took two wives, breaking the pattern of marriage God established with Adam and Eve.
    - ◆ He bragged about being a murderer.
    - ◆ He belittled God's protection of Cain by saying he (Lamech) would take eleven times the vengeance God provided for Cain on anyone who hurt him.
  - ▷ Lamech's son Jabal was credited with being the father of the nomads who lived in tents and owned livestock.
  - ▷ Lamech's son Jubal invented musical instruments and developed music.
  - ▷ Lamech's son Tubal-Cain was a master craftsman in both bronze and iron.
- ▶ The line of Seth (Adam and Eve's third son), was marked by their proclamation of the Lord (*Gen. 4:25-5:20*). They were a family who faithfully witnessed and testified to the goodness of God.
  - ▷ Adam, Seth's father, lived 930 years and fathered other sons and daughters after Seth.
  - ▷ Seth himself lived 912 years and fathered other sons and daughters after Enosh, his first son.

NOTES

NOTES

- ▷ Enosh lived 905 years and fathered other children after Cainan, his first son.
- ▷ Cainan lived 910 years and fathered other children after Mahalaleel, his first son.
- ▷ Mahalaleel lived 895 years and fathered other children after Jared, his first son.
- ▷ Jared lived 962 years and fathered other children after Enoch, his first son.
- ▶ The Bible says Enoch was a man who "walked with God." He was the father of Methuselah, the oldest man who ever lived (*Gen. 5:21-27*).
    - ▷ Enoch is one of only two men who the Bible says walked with God before the Flood. The other is his great-grandson Noah (*Gen. 6:9*).
    - ▷ Enoch is noted in the New Testament as one of the heroes of faith (*Heb. 11:5*).
    - ▷ The New Testament says that Enoch was a powerful prophet who spoke about coming judgment. His message can be found in *Jude 1:14-15*.
    - ▷ Enoch is one of two human beings who entered heaven without going through a physical death (*Gen. 5:24*).
    - ▷ Enoch's life on earth lasted 365 years.
    - ▷ Enoch's son Methuselah lived 969 years. Enoch's first son was Lamech. Enoch also fathered other children.
    - ▷ Lamech lived 777 years. Lamech's first son was Noah, who was famous as the faithful man of the Flood. Lamech also fathered other children.
    - ▷ Noah was 500 years old when he fathered his sons Shem, Ham, and Japheth. It is at this point where the story of the Flood begins.

C. **The Flood** (*Gen. 6-9*)
- Before the Flood, people and their wickedness multiplied on the earth (*Gen. 6:1-5*).
- Their wickedness became so great that God made the decision to destroy man (*Gen. 6:6-7*).
- God informed Noah of His decision to destroy the earth with a flood, and directed Noah to build an ark (*Gen. 6:8-22*).
    - ▶ Noah walked with God, so he and his family would survive.
    - ▶ Noah was to take two (male and female) of every animal and bird on the ark to keep their species alive; and seven each of every clean animal and birds of the air (see *Gen. 7:2-3*).
    - ▶ Noah built the ark God had directed.

Questions:

Describe the attitudes and actions that made Noah different than the others who were on the earth at the time of the Flood. Use Scripture to support your answers.

What attitudes and actions make you different than those people around you who do not have a relationship with Jesus Christ?

NOTES

- Noah, his family, and the animals entered the ark (*Gen. 7:1-10*).
- Forty days and nights of a very strong rain combined with "the fountains of the deep," to cause a flood that lasted for another 150 days.
  - ▶ The waters covered even the mountains by over six meters.
  - ▶ Every living thing on land was destroyed.
- The flood ends (*Gen. 8:1-19*).
  - ▶ The ark rested on a mountain called Ararat.
  - ▶ Noah sent out a raven and then a dove (twice), to help determine if there was dry land again.
  - ▶ A full year after the Flood began, the waters returned to the rivers, lakes and oceans as they had been before.
    - ▷ God invited Noah and his family to come off the ark.
    - ▷ God commanded Noah to bring out the animals from the ark.
- Noah worshiped God by sacrificing clean animals and clean birds (Gen. 8:20-22).
  - ▶ God recognized the evil in man's heart, but promised not to curse the ground or destroy every living thing again.
  - ▶ God confirmed the order of seasons, and day and night.
- God made a covenant with Noah confirmed by the rainbow (*Gen. 9:1-17*).
  - ▶ God commanded Noah's family to repopulate the earth.
  - ▶ God announced that animals would fear and be subject to man.
  - ▶ God permitted animals to become a part of man's diet.
    - ▷ Even here God banned eating flesh with blood in it, just as He would command in the laws He gave Moses.
  - ▶ God demanded the life of any man who murders another.
  - ▶ God promised never to destroy the earth with a flood again.
  - ▶ The rainbow was the sign to remind everyone of the covenant between God, Noah, all mankind, and every creature.
- Noah's family became divided by sin (*Gen. 9:18-29*).
  - ▶ After the flood, Noah became a farmer with a vineyard.
  - ▶ One day Noah became drunk on wine from his vineyard. While drunk, he exposed himself inside his tent. As a result, with being seen Noah was shamed by this.
    - ▷ Noah's son Ham and his grandson Canaan viewed Noah's nakedness.
    - ▷ Noah's sons Shem and Japheth refused to look on Noah's nakedness and covered their father with a blanket while looking away from him.
  - ▶ When Noah recovered he found out about the shame Ham and Canaan caused him.
    - ▷ Noah cursed Canaan to be a servant of the rest of the family. In this way, he shamed Ham.
    - ▷ At the same time, Noah blessed Shem and Japheth.
  - ▶ Noah died at age 950.

NOTES

- When Noah died, his family was divided. Still, their task was to repopulate the earth.

D. **Human Chaos** (*Gen. 10-11*)
- The origins of nations can be traced back to the sons of Noah, whose descendents settled the ancient world (*Gen. 10; 11:10-32*).
  - Some of the descendants of Japheth (listed below), are believed to be the founders of the nations next to their names.
    - Gomer (Germany)
    - Magog, Tubal, and Mechech (Russia)
    - Madai (Persia)
    - Javan (Greece)
    - Tiras (Italy)
    - Togarmah (Armenia)
    - Tarshish (Spain)
    - Kittim (Cyprus)
  - Some of the descendants of Ham (listed below) are believed to be the founders of the nations next to their names.
    - Cush (Ethiopia)
    - Mizraim (Egypt)
    - Phut (Africa)
    - Canaan (the Canaanites of Palestine)
    - Nimrod (Babylon and Assyria)
    - Sidon (Phoenicia)
    - Heth (Hittites)
    - Jebus (the Jebusites, who occupied Jerusalem prior to David)
    - Pilistim (the Philistines)
    - Sin (the possible founder of China, Japan, India and other oriental nations)
  - The descendants of Shem are less scattered.
    - The nation Israel came through Abraham, Isaac, and Jacob.
    - The Middle East Arab countries came through Abraham, Ishmael, and Esau.[3]
  - Some scholars believe that the family line of Ham contributed technical proficiency to man. The line of Japheth contributed especially to science and philosophy. Shem's family line produced Abraham, and later Jesus. His family line is credited with religious insights that produced spiritual health.
- Mankind went into confusion and chaos at the Tower of Babel (*Gen. 11:1-9*).
  - Nimrod, the grandson of Ham, led the building of a tower that would be both a city and a place to study astrology.
    - The purpose of the tower was to "make a name" for its builders, not to glorify God.
  - God punishes this effort by confusing their speech. The result is the people's division into groups with many languages, making it impossible to continue building the tower.
  - The name "Babel," by which the tower and city became known, literally means "confusion."
- The Bible account of the Creation Stage ends with the family line of Abraham, with whom the Patriarchal Stage begins.

Questions:

1) List the differences between Cain and Abel. Support your answer with Scripture.

2) Read about the Tower of Babel in *Genesis 11*. Have you ever done something to make a name for yourself? What was the result?

3) Find three things in *Genesis 1* and *2* showing that God created man to be different from the animals.

Chapter Two
The Patriarchal Stage

1. Patriarchal Stage Overview

A. The Patriarchal Stage covers the time from 2165-1804 BC (*Genesis 12-50* and *Job*).
   - This stage begins with the life of Abraham, and ends at the death of Joseph.

B. The key people in the Patriarchal Stage are: Abraham, Isaac, Jacob, Joseph, and Job.

C. The key events in the Patriarchal Stage include: the beginning of the Hebrew nation, the covenant between God and Abraham, the Jews moving into Egypt, and God allowing Satan to test Job.

D. The locations of the key events in this stage are:
   - The beginning of the Hebrew nation and the covenant with Abraham: Canaan.
   - The Jews moving into Egypt: Canaan, then Egypt.
   - God allowing Satan to test Job: Uz (present day North Arabia).

E. There are several important details in this stage.
   - The birth of Ishmael to Abraham and Sarah's maid Hagar. Ishmael became the father of the Arab peoples in the Middle East today (*Gen. 16*).
   - God destroys Sodom and Gomorrah for its evil (*Gen. 19*).
   - Isaac's son Esau gives away his birthright as the firstborn, which gave him rights to double the share of Isaac's estate and God's blessing, for a bowl of stew (*Gen. 25*).

2. The Bible Account of the Patriarchal Stage

A. **Abraham** (*Gen. 12-24*; about 2166-1991 BC)
   - Abraham was called "Abram" until he was 99 years old. God changed Abram's name based on a covenant promise (see *Gen. 17:1-8*).
     ▶ Abram grew up in the city of Ur in southern Mesopotamia. Ur was located on the Euphrates River. It was a prosperous trading center.
     ▶ People in Ur worshiped many gods, but the main god of the city was the moon god Sin.
     ▶ God established His covenant with His people through Abraham.
     ▶ The Hebrew people trace themselves and their faith back to Abraham.
   - Abram and his family had settled in Haran on their way to Canaan. God told Abram to leave Haran and finish the journey to Canaan. Before Abram began that journey, God made seven promises to him (*Gen. 12:1-4*).
     ▶ To make Abram the father of a great nation.
     ▶ To bless Abram.

NOTES

- ▶ To make Abram's name great.
- ▶ To make Abram a blessing.
- ▶ To bless those who blessed Abram.
- ▶ To curse those who cursed Abram.
- ▶ To bless the families of all the earth through Abram.
* When Abram arrived in Canaan, he built an altar to the Lord. The Lord promised Abram the land (*Gen. 12:4-9*).
* A famine caused Abram to leave Canaan and go to Egypt. While in Egypt, Abram lied about his marriage to Sarai his wife. He deceived Pharaoh to think that Sarai was only his sister, so the Pharaoh took Sarai into his house. Abram's lie had seven bad results (*Gen. 12:10-20*):
  - ▶ Abram disappointed God.
  - ▶ Abram weakened his own faith.
  - ▶ Abram weakened Sarai's faith.
  - ▶ Abram set a bad example for his nephew Lot.
  - ▶ Abram caused the Pharaoh to be hurt with great plagues.
  - ▶ Abram and Sarai picked up Hagar. This is the Egyptian handmaid with whom Abram would have a son and try to fulfill God's promise ahead of God's timing.
  - ▶ Abram set a bad example that his son Isaac would copy years later.

Question:

Even though Abram lied about being married to Sarai, God protected their marriage and continued to lead Abram on his journey. What does this say about the importance of the covenant between God and Abram? Use Scripture to support your answer.

* Abram and his nephew Lot needed to graze their livestock on different lands so there would be enough food for both herds. Lot chose the plain of Jordan. Abram settled in Hebron, where he built another altar to honor God (*Gen. 13*).
* Lot was kidnapped by a group of foreign kings, who also took the wealth of Sodom and Gomorrah. Abram chased the kings and recovered Lot and the stolen wealth of Sodom and Gomorrah. After his victory, Abram met Melchizedek (*Gen. 14*). There were four important details to remember from this meeting:
  - ▶ It was the first communion.
  - ▶ It has the first mention of Jerusalem, which back then was called "Salem." Jeru (city of), Salem (peace).
  - ▶ It was the first mention of a priest. Melchizedek was the priest of the Most High God.
  - ▶ It was the first mention of a tithe. Here, Abram gave a tithe to Melchizedek as though he were giving to the Lord.

NOTES

- At the close of this meeting, the king of Sodom offered to give Abram the wealth he had recovered for Sodom. Abram refused, wanting only the wealth God provided (*Gen. 14:22-24*).
- God then confirmed His covenant with Abram through a blood agreement of animal sacrifice. He confirmed that Abram would inherit Canaan, and that Abram would be the father of a great nation. This was an unconditional covenant. God would make it happen (*Gen. 15*).
- During this event, God told Abram about the 400-year captivity of Israel in Egypt. He also told Abram that his descendents would come back to Canaan.
- Abram still had no physical son of his own to be his heir. God had promised to provide an heir through Abram's body (*Gen. 16*).
  - ▶ Sarai thought an heir could be provided through Hagar, her maidservant. Hagar became Abram's wife, and soon became pregnant.
  - ▶ Hagar began looking down on Sarai because Sarai couldn't have children. Sarai became angry with Hagar. Finally Hagar ran away.
  - ▶ God's angel told Hagar to return to Sarai and have the child. Ishmael was born to Abraham and Hagar.
- God gave Abram and Sarai new names as He made the covenant clearer to them. When Abram was 99, God changed Abram's name to "Abraham" which means "father of nations." God also changed Sarai's name to "Sarah" which means "a princess" (*Gen. 17*).
  - ▶ God said that Sarah would become a mother of nations. Abraham laughed at the news because he was 100 years old, and Sarah was 90 years old. They were both well past the age of having children.
  - ▶ God said that circumcision would be the sign of His covenant from that day forward. Abraham circumcised himself, Ishmael, and all the men of his house that day.
  - ▶ God also said that Sarah would bear a son they would name Isaac at the same time the next year.
- God and two angels visited Abraham at Mamre in Hebron. They told Abraham that he and Sarah would have their heir the next spring. They also told Abraham about the Lord's plan to destroy Sodom and Gomorrah because of the great sin in those cities (*Gen. 18-19*).
  - ▶ God agreed with Abraham to spare the cities if there were just ten righteous people in Sodom, but even that number could not be found.
  - ▶ Sodom and Gomorrah were destroyed as Lot and his family fled Sodom.
- Lot's wife looked back at the cities and she became a pillar of salt. In *Luke 17:32*, Jesus said to "remember Lot's wife" as a warning against becoming devoted to earthly things.
- A famine once again drove Abraham from Canaan. He went to Philistia and again lied about his marriage to Sarah (*Gen. 20*).
  - ▶ God spared the Philistine king Abimelech by warning him in a dream that Sarah was Abraham's wife.
  - ▶ Abimelech gave Abraham and Sarah livestock, servants, and choice land to use as a result of this event.
- That spring, Isaac was born to Abraham and Sarah. As a result, Hagar and Ishmael were sent away. Yet God promised that Ishmael would also become a great nation (*Gen. 21*).

- After several years, God told Abraham to sacrifice Isaac. Abraham was completely obedient to the point of striking Isaac dead, when God stopped Abraham and supplied a substitute ram for Isaac. For his obedience, Abraham was again promised a great number of descendants (*Gen. 22*).
  - ▶ This event took place at Mt. Moriah. Mt. Moriah is sometimes suggested to be Golgotha, the same place where Jesus was crucified (*Mat. 27:33*).
  - ▶ Abraham gave God a new name: <u>Jehovah-Jireh</u>, which means "the Lord will provide."
- Abraham's wife Sarah died at age 127 and was buried in the cave of Machpelah (*Gen. 23*).
- Abraham secured a wife for Isaac through a servant. The servant prayed to be shown the right woman, and God answered that Rebekah was that woman (*Gen. 24*).
- Abraham married Keturah, who bore him six sons. The fourth was Midian, the father of the Midianites (*Gen. 25:1-6*).
- Abraham died at age 175, and was buried with Sarah in the cave of Machpelah (*Gen. 25:7-10*).

B. **Isaac** (*Gen. 25-27*; about 2066-1886 BC)
  - Isaac was not as powerful a patriarch as his father Abraham or son Jacob. Yet he shows himself to be a hard worker and a praying parent. His story takes place almost entirely near Hebron in Canaan.
  - As a boy, Isaac showed himself to be a trusting son as he was offered up for sacrifice by his father Abraham (*Gen. 22:1-4*).
  - As a husband, Isaac was known for his love for Rebekah (*Gen.24:62-67*).
  - Isaac was a praying man. He prayed that God would bless Rebekah and him with children. God answered and Rebekah gave birth to the twins Jacob and Esau. They would struggle against each other for many years (*Gen. 25:19-26*).
  - Isaac copied the sin of his father Abraham. He also lied about being married. (*Gen. 26:1-11*).
    - ▶ When famine drove Isaac to journey to Philistia, Isaac told the king there that Rebekah was his sister. The lie was discovered when Isaac and Rebekah were caught sharing an intimate moment. The king of Philistia ordered that no one touch Isaac or Rebekah.
  - Isaac showed that God had blessed him through prospering his land and livestock. The Philistines around him were jealous of his prosperity, and filled up his father Abraham's wells with trash. Isaac cleaned out the wells and dug them again. This led to even greater prosperity for Isaac and a source of water for his people and others (*Gen. 26:17-33*).
  - As an adult, Isaac is remembered most as the father of Jacob and Esau (*Gen. 27:1-45*).
    - ▶ Once Isaac felt he was near death. He asked Esau to prepare a meal of wild game for him. Then Isaac would give Esau his birthright blessing.
    - ▶ While Esau was off hunting, Rebekah disguised Jacob so Isaac (who had very weak eyes) would give Jacob the birthright blessing. Jacob received Isaac's blessing intended for Esau.

NOTES

> ▶ After Isaac found out what had happened, Isaac sent Jacob away to find a wife and to avoid Esau.
- Isaac lived for another 43 years after he was deceived by Jacob and Rebekah. He died at the age of 180 and was buried at Mamre in Hebron (*Gen. 35:27-28*).

C. **Jacob** (*Gen. 28-36*; about 2006-1859 BC)
- Jacob is known for wrestling with God in prayer one night. God changes his name to Israel as a result. Jacob's twelve sons are the fathers of the twelve tribes of Israel, including Judah, from whose family line came the Messiah.
- Jacob received the patriarchal birthright out of trickery.
  - ▶ He convinced his brother Esau into trading his birthright for a bowl of stew (*Gen. 25:27-34*).
  - ▶ Years later, he would trick his father Isaac into believing he was Esau. Half-blind Isaac gave the birthright blessing to Jacob as a result (*Gen. 27:6-29*).
- While he traveled to escape Esau and find a bride, Jacob dreamed he saw a ladder at Bethel (*Gen. 28:10-22*).
  - ▶ The ladder led from earth to heaven. Angels were moving up and down the ladder.
  - ▶ In the dream, God make the same covenant promises to Jacob as He did to Abraham.
  - ▶ When Jacob awoke, he anointed a pile of rocks and vowed to serve God.
- Jacob met his future wife Rachel beside a well (*Gen. 29:21-30:24*).
  - ▶ He promised Rachel's father Laban that he would work seven years in exchange for Rachel being his wife.
  - ▶ But on the night he was to be married to Rachel, Laban substituted her older sister Leah for Rachel.
  - ▶ Jacob was angry, but agreed to work another seven years for Laban so he could marry Rachel.

Question:

How did Jacob show his love for Rachel over the years they knew each other? (Look also at the story of Joseph in *Gen. 37-50* for more hints.) Use Scripture to support your answers.

  - ▶ This gave Jacob two wives. Because Rachel and Leah also gave Jacob their handmaidens for childbearing, Jacob ended up with four wives. Between them, they bore the twelve sons who would father the twelve tribes of Israel.

- ▷ Leah bore: Reuben, Simeon, Levi, Judah, Issachar, Zebulun, and a daughter Dinah.
- ▷ Bilhah, Rachel's handmaid, bore: Dan and Naphtali.
- ▷ Zilpah, Leah's handmaid, bore: Gad and Asher.
- ▷ Rachel bore: Joseph and Benjamin.
- Jacob and Laban went into business together. Jacob became a wealthy man. God told Jacob to return to his home, and Jacob left without telling Laban (*Gen. 30:25-31:55*).
    - ▶ Laban chased Jacob down and accused Jacob of thievery.
    - ▶ The men settled their argument and made a memorial pile of stones to remember their truce.
- Jacob still had an uneasy relationship with Esau. Jacob heard Esau was riding with 400 men to meet with him. Jacob was filled with fear (*Gen. 32:1-33:20*).
    - ▶ Jacob wrestled in prayer with God all night.
    - ▶ God reassured Jacob and changed Jacob's name to Israel, which means "one who has struggled with God." Jacob's meeting with Esau was pleasant.
- Jacob's children were not always righteous.
    - ▶ His sons Levi and Simeon committed murder to pay back a group of desert men whose leader had sexual relations with their sister Dinah (*Gen. 34:1-31*).
    - ▶ His son Reuben committed adultery with Rachel's handmaiden Bilhah, who was only to have relations with Jacob (*Gen. 35:22*).
    - ▶ His son Judah committed adultery with his own daughter-in-law (*Gen. 38:1-30*).
- Jacob himself tried to turn his family back toward God (*Gen. 35:1-15*).
    - ▶ God ordered Jacob back to Bethel. To prepare for the trip, Jacob ordered his household to destroy their idols and prepare their hearts.
    - ▶ Once they arrived at Bethel, Jacob built an altar and called it "El Bethel," meaning "the God of the house of God."
- As Jacob grew older, he was sorrowful over the loss of loved ones.
    - ▶ Rebekah died during the birth of their son Benjamin (*Gen. 35:16-20*).
    - ▶ His father Isaac died at the age of 180. Jacob and Esau buried Isaac alongside Abraham at Hebron in the cave of Machpelah (*Gen. 35:27-29*).
    - ▶ His older sons convinced Jacob that Joseph was killed by a wild beast (*Gen. 37:31-35*).

D. **Joseph** (*Gen. 37-50*; around 1914-1804 BC)
- Joseph was the eleventh of Jacob's twelve sons. He began life in Canaan helping his family herd flocks, and ended up as an Egyptian official who was responsible for bringing Israel into Egypt.
- Jacob gave Joseph a coat of many colors to show that Joseph was his favorite son. Joseph also told his older brothers about dreams where his brothers bowed down to him (*Gen. 37*).
    - ▶ His older brothers didn't like the dreams or Joseph. They worked together to sell him into slavery.
    - ▶ Once Joseph was sold and on his way to Egypt, his brothers soaked Joseph's coat in blood. They took it to Jacob and tricked him into be-

NOTES

NOTES

lieving Joseph had been killed and eaten by a wild animal. Jacob was heartbroken.
- As a slave in Egypt, Joseph became a faithful servant in the house of Potiphar. God blessed the household to show favor to Joseph (*Gen. 39*).
  - Potiphar's wife tried to convince Joseph to have relations with her, but Joseph refused.
  - One time Potiphar's wife grabbed Joseph's garment and held on while Joseph ran. The garment stayed in her hand. She said it was proof that Joseph had tried to have relations with her.
  - Potiphar put Joseph into prison. Yet, God blessed Joseph as a leader there, too. Joseph was soon put in charge of the entire prison administration.
- Joseph was in prison with the Pharaoh's servant and baker (*Gen. 40*). They had strange dreams.
  - Joseph told them that the meaning of dreams belong to God. He then told them the meaning of their dreams, and his words came true. The servant was set free in three days, and the baker was put to death.
  - When the servant was set free, he forgot about Joseph.
- When the Pharaoh had a disturbing dream, his chief servant remembered Joseph. Joseph said God would give the Pharaoh an answer (*Gen. 41*).
  - God gave Joseph the meaning of the Pharaoh's dream, which told that seven years of plenty in Egypt would be followed by seven years of famine.
  - The Pharaoh chose Joseph as second in command of Egypt.
  - Joseph helped gather and store food during the years of plenty so Egypt would have food in the seven years of famine.
- The famine reached Joseph's family in Canaan. Joseph's older brothers came to Egypt and had to bargain with Joseph for food (*Gen. 42-44*).
  - Joseph recognized his brothers, but they did not recognize him.
  - At first Joseph was very angry at his brothers. Then Joseph used the situation to find out news of his father Jacob and younger brother Benjamin.
  - Joseph finally agreed to let them to return to Canaan with food for the family if Simeon remained in Egypt and the brothers brought Benjamin back with them.
  - Joseph gave them more tests of character to see if they had really changed. Their actions and words proved they had.
- Joseph revealed who he was to his brothers and forgave them. He welcomed them to live close to him in Egypt (*Gen. 45-48*).
  - Joseph asked that they tell Jacob about his position in Egypt, and to bring Jacob to Egypt quickly.
  - God told Jacob to go to Egypt, and he went with his sons and household.
  - Jacob asked to be buried in Canaan and not in Egypt.
  - Jacob then blessed Joseph's sons and Joseph.
- Jacob then gave his last words to his twelve sons. Joseph kept his word and buried Jacob in Canaan (*Gen. 49-50*).
  - Joseph reassured his brothers that they could stay in Egypt and he would provide for them.
  - Joseph died at the age of 110, and was buried in Egypt.

- The famine caused Israel to move into Egypt, where they stayed until the time of Moses and the Exodus.
- There are a number of similarities between the life of Joseph and the life of Jesus. Please refer to the following chart.[4]

Joseph and Jesus Compared

JOSEPH	LIKENESS	JESUS
Genesis 37:3	Beloved by their fathers	*Matthew 3:17*
Genesis 37:2	Saw themselves as shepherds	*John 10:11-14*
Genesis 37:13-14	Sent by their fathers to their brothers	*Luke 10:13; Hebrews 2:12*
Genesis 37:4-5, 8	Hated by their brothers without a cause	*John 1:11; 7:5; 15:25*
Genesis 37:20	Plotted against by their brothers	*John 11:53*
Genesis 39:7	Severely tempted	*Matthew 4:1*
Genesis 37:26	Taken to Egypt	*Matthew 2:14-15*
Genesis 37:23	Stripped of their robes	*John 19:23-24*
Genesis 37:28	Sold for the price of a slave	*Matthew 26:15*
Genesis 39:20	Bound	*Matthew 27:2*
Genesis 39:20	Remained silent: offered no self-defense	*Isaiah 53:7*
Genesis 39:16-18	Falsely accused	*Matthew 26:59-60*
Genesis 39:2, 21, 23	Experienced God's presence through everything	*John 16:32*
Genesis 41:41	Both highly exalted after their sufferings	*Philippians 2:9-11*

E. **Job** (*Job 1-42.* Date is in patriarchal times; possibly the earliest among the patriarchs)
- Job is an historical figure who is typically famous for his trials. He is mentioned by both Ezekiel (*Eze. 14:14, 20*) and James (*Jam. 5:11*). The land of Uz may have been northeast of the Sea of Galilee, stretching toward the Euphrates River. Yet we do not have as many of the details in history that we have about the other patriarchs.
- Job's trials began when Satan challenged his motives for worshiping God (*Job 1-2*).
  ▶ Satan said that Job would curse God and die if Job lost his wealth.
  ▶ God said Job would remain faithful, and allowed Satan to test Job's faith through five trials.
    ▷ Job's farmhands were killed and his oxen and donkeys stolen.
    ▷ Job's sheep and herdsmen were burned by fire.
    ▷ Job's servants were killed and his camels stolen.
    ▷ A mighty wind killed Job's children.
    ▷ Job was stricken with boils.

NOTES

- Job's wife made his situation worse. She encouraged Job to curse God and die (*Job 2:9*).
- Job's friends were little help to him. Without seeking God's advice first, they tried to advise Job.
  - ▶ Eliphaz (*Job 4, 5, 15, 22*), based his advice on personal experience. He said that Job was suffering because of the sin of pride, and his sin against the poor and hungry.
  - ▶ Bildad (*Job 8, 18, 25*), based his advice on tradition. He also said that Job was suffering because of his sin. He told Job to repent.
  - ▶ Zophar (*Job 11, 20*), based his advice on what he thought were expert opinions. He also said that Job was suffering because of his sin, and told Job to repent.
  - ▶ Elihu (*Job 32-37*), based his advice on his own wisdom. He said Job was suffering because Job spoke foolishly. He accused Job of false righteousness. He finally asked Job to consider God's glory and greatness.
- Job responded to his friends in nine separate speeches
  - ▶ In these nine speeches Job talks about several topics.
    - ▷ Righteousness and suffering (*27:6; 31:1-40*).
    - ▷ Good works (*29:12-17; 30:25*).
    - ▷ Health, wealth and respect (*29:1-11, 20-25*).
    - ▷ Unfair punishment (*9:16-17, 30-33; 10:2, 7-8; 13:26-27; 19:6-11; 30:20-21*).
    - ▷ Friends (*12:2; 13:4; 16:2; 19:3*).
    - ▷ "Try being in my place" (*16:4-5*).
    - ▷ Answers (*28:12-28*).
    - ▷ God (*23:8-9*).
    - ▷ Trusting God (*13:15; 16:19; 23:10*).
- God asked Job two sets of questions.
  - ▶ The First Set of Questions (*Job 38-39*).
    - ▷ Where were you when I laid the earth's foundations? (*38:4*)
    - ▷ Do you know how big the earth is? (*38:18*)
    - ▷ Where do light and darkness dwell? (*38:19*)
    - ▷ How is the light parted that scatters the east wind upon the earth? (*38:24*)
    - ▷ Who fathered the rain and dew? (*38:28*)
    - ▷ Can you teach God anything? (*40:2*)
  - ▶ The Second Set of Questions (*Job 40:6-41:33*)
    - ▷ Have you thought about how big the hippopotamus I created is? (*40:15*)
    - ▷ Are you able to fish for sea monsters? (*41:1*)
- God's questions led Job to repent (*Job 42*).
  - ▶ God restores Job.
    - ▷ Job is allowed to see God's glory.
    - ▷ Job sees himself as God sees him.
    - ▷ Job is justified by God before his friends.
    - ▷ Job's health is fully restored.
    - ▷ Job is comforted by his sister and brothers.
    - ▷ Job is given double his former wealth.
    - ▷ Job is given seven more sons and three more daughters.

▷ Job lives to enjoy his grandchildren and great-grandchildren with 140 additional years of life.
- Why did Job suffer? Here are a few reasons.
  ▶ To silence Satan (*Job 1:9-11; 2:4, 5*).
  ▶ To see God (*Job 42:5*).
  ▶ To see himself (*Job 40:4; 42:6*).
  ▶ To help his friends learn not to judge (*Job 42:7*).
  ▶ To learn to pray for his friends (*Job 42:10*).
  ▶ To show that all things finally work together for good if you belong to God (*Job 42:10*; see *Rom. 8:28*).

Questions:

Have you been in a situation where, like Job, you tried to teach God something? What were the results?

Find one thing about each of the patriarchs that you believe sets a good example for godly leaders. Write the place in the Bible where you find each one.

1) Abraham

2) Isaac

3) Jacob

4) Joseph

5) Job

NOTES

CHAPTER THREE
THE EXODUS STAGE

1. Exodus Stage Overview

A. The Exodus Stage covers the time from 1804-1405 BC, and the books of Exodus, Leviticus, Numbers and Deuteronomy.
  - This stage begins with the death of Joseph, and ends with the death of Moses.

B. The key people in the Exodus Stage are: Moses, Aaron, Miriam, Eleazer, Korah, Balaam, Phineas, Caleb and Joshua.

C. The key events in the Exodus Stage are: Israel's deliverance from Egypt, the building of the tabernacle, the giving of the Law of Moses, Israel's failure at Kadesh-Barnea, and Israel's wandering in the wilderness.

D. The locations of the key events in this stage are:
  - Israel's deliverance from Egypt: Egypt and the Sinai wilderness.
  - The building of the tabernacle: Mt. Sinai.
  - The giving of the Law of Moses: Mt. Sinai.
  - Israel's failure at Kadesh-Barnea: near the Promised Land.
  - Israel's wandering through the wilderness: the wilderness areas of Sinai, Paran, Moab, Edom, and Ammon.

E. There are other important activities in this stage.
  - God provides manna for Israel (*Exo. 16:14*).
  - God commands the keeping of the Sabbath (*Exo. 16:23-30*).
  - God gives the Ten Commandments to His people (*Exo. 20:3-17*).
  - Joshua is chosen as Israel's new leader (*Num. 20:7-13; Deu. 34:9*).

2. The Bible Account of the Exodus Stage

A. **Israel: Slavery in Egypt** (*Exo. 1-12:36*; about 1804-1446 BC)
  - Sometime after Joseph died, the Pharaohs in Egypt forgot about who he was. They also forgot that Israel began their time in Egypt as welcomed guests. They treated the people of Israel as slaves. The mistreatment grew worse as the number of Israelites in Egypt grew (*Exo. 1*).
    ▸ The Pharaohs who forgot Joseph and turned the Israelites into slaves were those of the Hyksos Period (about 1730-1570 BC).
    ▸ The Pharaohs who took Moses into their palace were from the Eighteenth Dynasty. Thutmose I, Thutmose II, Queen Hatshepsut and Thutmose III ruled during the first 80 years of Moses' life (about 1527-1447 BC).[5]
  - God remembered His covenant with Abraham. Israel's people were Abraham's descendants. He heard Israel's cries and prayers for their freedom from Egypt (*Exo. 2:23-25*).

- Moses, the man God would use to deliver Israel from Egypt, was born about 1527 BC. As a baby, he was rescued from the Nile River by an Egyptian princess (*Exo. 2:1-14*).
  ▶ Moses grew up as a prince in Egypt for the first 40 years of his life.
  ▶ While he was rescuing an Israeli slave, he struck and killed an Egyptian guard. Moses ran away from Egypt to the wilderness in Midian.
- Moses spent his next 40 years as a shepherd in Midian (*Exo. 2:15-4:31*).
  ▶ Here, Moses married Zipporah.
  ▶ God called Moses to deliver His people from Egypt by speaking to Moses in a burning bush.
  ▶ Moses returned to Egypt to fulfill God's call.
- Moses went to Pharaoh and asked him to free Israel. Pharaoh refused to free Israel, and increased their work load (*Exo. 5:2, 4-9*).
  ▶ The Pharaoh at this time is believed to be Amenhotep II, who ruled Egypt from about 1447-1421 BC.
- God sent ten plagues on Egypt to show Pharaoh that he needed to free Israel (*Exo. 7-10*). The plagues showed Israel their true God, and Egypt their false gods.[6]

The Plague	*Egyptian God Defeated*	*Scripture Reference*
Water into blood	Osiris	*Exo. 7:20*
Frogs	Hekt	*Exo. 8:6*
Lice	Seb	*Exo. 8:17*
Flies	Hatkok	*Exo. 8:24*
Cattle disease	Apis	*Exo. 9:6*
Boils	Typhon	*Exo. 9:10*
Hail with fire	Shu	*Exo. 9:24*
Locusts	Serapia	*Exo. 10:13*
Three-day darkness	Ra	*Exo. 10:22*
Death of firstborn	All gods	*Exo. 12:29*

- After the final plague took the firstborn of all the unprotected homes, including his own, the Pharaoh released the Israelites (*Exo. 12:31-32*).
- God told Moses to lead the Israelites to Canaan by the southern route to avoid conflicts in the region (*Exo. 13:17-18*).
  ▶ Moses took the bones of Joseph with them to Canaan as Joseph had requested (*Exo. 13:19; Gen. 50:24-25*).

B. **Israel: On the Way to Mt. Sinai** (*Exo. 12:37-18:27*; about 1446 B.C.)
- When Israel left Egypt and began its wilderness journey, God provided a pillar of cloud by day and a pillar of fire by night to lead them (*Exo. 13:21-22*).
- The Pharaoh changed his mind about releasing the Israelites. He went after Israel with his army to capture them (*Exo. 14:5-10*).

NOTES
- ▶ The Israelites complained and accused Moses of leading them into the wilderness to die.
- ▶ Moses told them that God would save them. God told Moses to keep the people moving forward toward the Red Sea.
- God put the pillar of cloud and fire between the Egyptian army and the Israelites. This kept the Israelites safe as they entered the Red Sea, which God had parted so Israel could walk through the sea on dry ground (*Exo. 14:13-15:21*).
  - ▶ After Israel had passed through the parted Red Sea, God told Moses to stretch his hand toward the sea and close it on the Egyptian army. Moses did so, and the Egyptian army was destroyed.
  - ▶ Israel worshiped God for delivering them from Egypt.
    - ▷ The crossing of the Red Sea was a reason to worship God for generations to come, and even today. It is mentioned in *Psa. 78:53; 106:11-12, 22*; and *Heb. 11:29*.
- Three days after the Red Sea crossing, Israel ran out of water. They came across a bitter source of water at a place called Marah (*Exo. 15:22-26*).
  - ▶ God showed Moses a tree that would make the water sweet. Moses threw the tree into the water, and the water became drinkable.
  - ▶ God promised that if Israel would obey Him, He would not bring the diseases on them that He had brought on Egypt.
- The Israelites complained about how they would get food. God provided food for Israel while they traveled each day. It was white and tasted like honey on wafers. Israel called it "manna" (*Exo. 16:4, 14, 35*).
  - ▶ The manna appeared on the ground each morning. The people could only gather as much as they could eat at one time. This made them dependent on God for their daily bread.
  - ▶ Manna became Israel's staple diet for the next forty years.
- God told Moses to have Israel observe the Sabbath day of rest on the seventh day of the week (*Exo. 16:23, 26-30*).
- Israel continued its journey through the wilderness and found itself without water again at Rephidim (*Exo. 17:1-7*).
  - ▶ The people complained and threatened Moses.
  - ▶ God told Moses to strike a rock that would provide water. Moses obeyed, and the rock produced the needed water.
  - ▶ Even after God's provision of food and water, Israel's faith in God was weak. They still asked if God was really with them or not. (*Exo. 17:7*).
- The Amalekites attacked Israel while Israel was camped at Rephidim. Israel won the battle with Joshua leading its army. Aaron and Hur supported Moses' arms as Moses held out his rod over the battle (*Exo. 17:8-16*).
  - ▶ God instructed Moses to write down what happened in a book. This may be a book that became part of the Bible.

C. **Israel: Camped at Sinai** (*Exo. 19:1-Num. 10:10*; about 1446 BC, three months after Israel left Egypt)
  - Three main events happened at Sinai that would define Israel's spiritual life.
    - ▶ The first was the giving of the Law, which described the requirements for fellowship with God.

- ▶ The second was Israel's worship of the golden calf, which broke their fellowship with God.
- ▶ The third was the construction of the tabernacle, which helped restore Israel's fellowship with God.
- The commandments of the Law, if obeyed, would keep Israel in fellowship with God and each other (*Exo. 20:3-17*).
  - ▶ The moral code in the Law was based on the Ten Commandments.
    - ▷ Have no gods before the true God.
    - ▷ Do not make graven images.
    - ▷ Do not take God's name in vain.
    - ▷ Keep the Sabbath.
    - ▷ Honor your father and mother.
    - ▷ Do not kill.
    - ▷ Do not commit adultery.
    - ▷ Do not steal.
    - ▷ Do not lie.
    - ▷ Do not covet.
  - ▶ The spiritual code in the Law dealt with special rules for the right worship of God. It includes the levitical feasts and offerings. It also points to Christ and His forgiveness (*Exo. 35-40; Leviticus*; see *1 Cor. 10:4*).
  - ▶ The social code in the Law had 70 basic rules about marriage, health, sanitation, military service, and other issues that would help shape Israel's society (*Leviticus*).
- Israel became impatient while they waited for Moses to bring God's law down from Mt. Sinai (*Exo. 32*).
  - ▶ Aaron made a calf out of their gold jewelry and they worshiped it instead of God.
  - ▶ When God corrected them through Moses, He made them drink the gold that they used in the calf.
- Israel needed a central place to offer sacrifices and to worship God as a nation. They constructed a tabernacle for those purposes (*Exo. 25-31; 35-40*).
  - ▶ The tabernacle also pointed to the work of Jesus Christ.
  - ▶ The tabernacle had three sections: the outer court, the inner court, and the Holy of Holies.
    - ▷ The outer court was like a fence. It was 45.7 meters long, 22.85 meters wide, and 2.28 meters high. It had a bronze altar and a bronze basin.
    - ▷ There was a tent within the outer court that was 13.7 meters long, 4.57 meters wide, and 4.57 meters high.
    - ▷ The tent had two rooms separated by a thick curtain.
      - ♦ The eastern tent room was called the inner court or Holy Place. It had a showbread table, a lamp stand, and incense altar.
      - ♦ The western tent room was called the Holy of Holies. It held the Ark of the Covenant.
        - → The Ark of the Covenant was a small box, made of acacia wood and gold that held the tablets of the Ten Commandments and other objects.
          - ↳ The Ark's height and depth were 71 cm by 71 cm, and

NOTES

NOTES

  its length was 114 cm.
- The lid of the Ark was made of solid gold and was called the "mercy seat."
- The high priest would enter the Holy of Holies on the Day of Atonement and sprinkle blood upon the mercy seat for the sins of Israel.[7]

▸ The tabernacle was made of gold, silver, bronze, animal cloth, acacia wood, and onyx stones. The people of Israel built it in six months.
▸ The priests of the tabernacle had to come from the tribe of Levi. They were anointed with water, oil, and blood.
- The High Priest of the tabernacle had to come from the line of Aaron from the tribe of Levi. His duties were to care for the physical needs of the tabernacle and the spiritual needs of the people.
 ▸ There were five offerings given in the tabernacle.
- Three offerings maintained fellowship with God. These were the burnt offering (*Lev. 1*), the meal offering (*Lev. 2*), and the peace offering (*Lev. 3*).
- Two offerings restored fellowship with God. These were the sin offering (*Lev. 4*) and the trespass offering (*Lev. 5*).
 ▸ There were nine holy feasts celebrated in the tabernacle.
- Three feasts spoke of God's creation. These were the weekly Sabbath, the seven-year Sabbath, and the fifty-year Sabbath.
- Six feasts spoke of God's forgiveness and restoration. These were the Passover, the First Fruits feast, Pentecost, the Feast of Trumpets, the Feast of Atonement, and the Tabernacle Feast.
 ▸ As the tabernacle was dedicated, God's glory cloud filled it (*Exo. 40:33-38*). Sadly, God's judgment also fell on Aaron's two wicked sons (*Lev. 10:1-11*).
 ▸ The first census of Israel during the Exodus was taken at the outset of their journey from Sinai to Kadesh-Barnea (*Num. 1*). The number of males, 20 years of age and older, who could go to war were counted. The total number of this census was 603,550.

D. **Israel: On the Way to Kadesh-Barnea from Sinai** (*Num. 10:11-12:16*; about 1445 BC)
- Moses tried to get his brother-in-law Hobab to guide the Israelites through the wilderness. Hobab refused at first, but then agreed (*Num. 10:29-31*). God continued to lead Israel faithfully with a pillar of cloud by day, and a pillar of fire by night (*Num. 10:34-36*).
- The people of Israel still complained about their wilderness journey. They complained that they wanted things to be like they were when they had been slaves in Egypt. To stop their complaints, God sent a fire that consumed some of them. Moses prayed, and God stopped the fire (*Num. 11:1-3*).
- The heavy burden of leadership caused Moses to be discouraged. He asked God for help. God told Moses to choose 70 men to help him. God gave them all the same mind and heart about leading Israel (*Num. 11:14-25*).
- The Israelites complained about God's provision of manna. They chose to eat quail that had blown in from the sea instead. God struck those who ate the quail with a plague (*Num. 11:31-34*).

NOTES

- Aaron and Miriam (Moses' brother and sister) spoke against Moses because he had married a woman from Ethiopia. God punished Miriam with leprosy. Aaron asked Moses to pray for her healing. After seven-day purification, Miriam was restored (*Num. 12*).

Questions:

Imagine you were traveling with the Israelites through the wilderness. Which event of this journey to this point would encourage you most about God's faithfulness, and why? Use Scripture to support your answer.

Which event would you most likely use as a warning to others to remember that God needed to be honored in every way possible, and why? Use Scripture to support your answer.

E. **Israel: At Kadesh-Barnea** (*Num. 13-14*)
   - Kadesh-Barnea was just outside of the Promised Land. When Israel arrived at Kadesh-Barnea, God told Moses to send spies into Canaan and scout the land He was about to give them. Two different reports came back (*Num. 13*).
     ▶ Ten of the twelve spies said that Israel could not take the land because the people there were too strong and too big.
     ▶ Two of the twelve spies said that Israel could take the land because the Lord was with them.
   - Even with the promise of God that they could take the land, Israel refused to enter Canaan. They said they would rather replace Moses with another leader and return to Egypt (*Num. 14:1-10*).
     ▶ The Israelites were about to stone Moses and his faithful leaders when the glory of the Lord filled the tabernacle and stopped them.
   - This was Israel's tenth rebellion against God. God told Israel they would be punished for their refusal to enter the Promised Land (*Num. 14:11-38*).
     ▶ *Heb. 3:7-19* refers to this event as a warning against unbelief and rebellion.
     ▶ Israel's bodies would fall in the wilderness.
     ▶ No one over 20 years of age (except Joshua and Caleb) would enter the Promised Land.
     ▶ Israel would wander the wilderness for 40 years, a year for each day the spies spent in the land.
     ▶ The ten spies who said Israel could not take the land would die of a plague.
   - Israel then left Kadesh-Barnea to begin 40 years in the wilderness.

NOTES

F. **Israel: From Kadesh to the Eastern Bank of Jordan** (*Numbers 14:40-36:16*; about 1444-1405 BC.)
- Israel changed its mind about entering the Promised Land. Against Moses' warning, they tried to take Canaan in their own strength. The Canaanites and Amalekites drove them away (*Num. 14:40-45*).
- Israel was not consistent in working out its obedience to the covenant (*Num. 15:32-36*).
  - ▶ Although they had refused to enter the Promised Land, they chose to take the Sabbath seriously. Moses and the congregation stoned a man who worked on the Sabbath in open rebellion against God's command.
- Korah, a descendant of Levi, gathered 250 men to rebel against Moses. God caused the earth to open up and swallow Korah and his followers for their rebellion (*Num. 16*).
  - ▶ After this event, some Israelites still complained. They accused Moses of killing God's people. So God sent a plague of judgment that would kill another 14,700 people.
    - ▷ Jude mentions this event in his epistle as a stern warning against apostasy (*Jude 11*).
- Moses and Aaron often had to defend their places as God's chosen leaders. To show His favor of Moses and Aaron, God ordered the leaders from each tribe to place a rod with his name on it in the tabernacle. Aaron did the same. God caused Aaron's rod to blossom with ripe almonds hanging from it (*Num. 17*).
- Even in the rules for worship, God responded to the needs of His people (*Num. 19*).
- As close to God as Moses was, Moses still sinned. God commanded Moses to make water come from a rock at Kadesh. Moses struck the rock instead. God told Moses that his disobedience would prevent him from leading Israel into the Promised Land (*Num. 20:7-13*).
- Israel asked Edom for permission to pass through their land. Edom refused, and sent armed men to enforce their decision (*Num. 20:14-22*).
  - ▶ The result was that Israel had to travel an extra 290 kilometers through the desert.
- God ordered Moses to strip Aaron of his priestly garments and place them on Aaron's son Eleazar. This was in preparation for Aaron's death. (*Num. 20:23-29*).
  - ▶ Aaron was 123 years old when he died. He was buried at Mt. Hor.
- To punish Israel's continued rebellion, God sent poisonous snakes into their camp. This event caused the people to repent. God provided healing through the people looking at a brass serpent (*Num. 21:5-9*).
  - ▶ Jesus spoke about this event as He talked with Nicodemus (see *Joh. 3:14-15*).
  - ▶ King Hezekiah ordered that the brass serpent be destroyed because years later (in 700 BC), people worshiped it (see *2 Kin. 18:4*).
- Just as Edom refused Israel's request to pass through its land, so did the Amorites. But this time Israel's armies fought the Amorites and won (*Num. 21:24*).
- A corrupt prophet named Balaam took a bribe from the king of Moab to curse Israel. Balaam tried to curse Israel four times. Every time he tried words of blessing came out of his mouth (*Num. 22-25*).

- Although Balaam failed in cursing Israel, he arranged for Moabite women to seduce Israel's men. This weakened Israel almost as much as a military defeat.
  - Three New Testament writers mention Balaam.
    - Peter in *2 Peter 2:15*.
    - Jude in *Jude 11*.
    - John in *Revelation 2:14*.
- Aaron's grandson Phineas, "the priest," saved Israel by executing a prince from the tribe of Simeon and his lover from Midian. This was a sign of God's judgment for the men of Israel joining with foreign women.
- A second census of Israel was taken as it prepared to enter the Promised Land. This time, the number of males aged 20 and older who could serve in the military was 601,730 (*Num. 26*).
  - No one in Israel was alive who had been over 20 at the time of the Kadesh rebellion except Moses, Caleb and Joshua.
- Moses showed God's concern for widows and orphans when he granted the request of five daughters. The daughters of Zelophehad had lost their father. Because there were no sons in their family, Moses gave them the right to inherit their father's land when the Promised Land would be divided (*Num. 27:1-11*).
- Moses' authority was transferred to Joshua, who would lead Israel into the Promised Land (*Num. 27:12-23*).
- God told Moses to select 1,000 warriors from each of the twelve tribes to go to battle against Midian. They were to be God's judgment against Midian for Midian's refusal to let Israel pass through their land. Israel won the victory over the Midianites (*Num. 31*).
- The Reubenites, Gadites, and half-tribe of Manasseh asked Moses permission to settle in Gilead, an area east of the Promised Land. Moses agreed with the condition that these tribes help defeat the Canaanites with the rest of Israel (*Num. 32*).
- Six cities of refuge were named to deal with those who accidentally killed others (*Num. 35*).
  - On the eastern side of the Jordan River, those cities were Bezer, Golan, and Ramoth.
  - On the western side of the Jordan in the Promised Land, those cities were Kadesh, Shechem, and Hebron.
  - These six were part of the 48 cities given to the Levites. The Levites did not receive a regular section of land as the other tribes did.
  - These cities were a refuge to all who killed someone accidentally. Their purpose was to provide these people a place to avoid the dead person's relatives.

G. **Israel: The Eastern Bank** (*Deuteronomy*; 1405 BC.)
  - At the eastern bank of the Jordan River, Moses delivered his farewell messages to Israel.
    - Moses' first message told about the covenant between God and Israel. It then told about the history of God and His acts on behalf of Israel during the Exodus from Egypt (*Deu. 1:1-4:43*).
    - Moses' second message told about the special rules of the covenant.

NOTES

NOTES

It also showed how the covenant would apply in the Promised Land (*Deu. 4:44-26:19*).

▶ Moses' third message told about the terms of the covenant. It also told about what would happen to Israel, in both the near and the distant future (*Deu. 27:1-30:20*).

- Moses spoke to Joshua before Israel about Joshua's duties as Israel's new leader (*Deu. 31:7-8, 14*).
- Moses blessed each of the twelve tribes (*Deu. 33:1-3; 27-29*).
- Moses also completed the first five books of the Bible (called the Pentateuch) at this time (see *Deu. 31:9, 24*).
- Moses composed and delivered a song of praise to God and warning to Israel to be faithful (*Deu. 32*).
- God directed Moses to go to Mt. Nebo, where Moses would see the Promised Land he would never enter.
   ▶ Moses was 120 years old when he died. He was buried somewhere in the plains of Moab.
- The Exodus was finished. Israel was prepared to take the Promised Land.

Questions:

Find three events in the Exodus Stage that show God's determination for Israel to reach the Promised Land. Write the events and where you found them in the Bible in the spaces below.

1)

2)

3)

God used a pillar of cloud by day and a pillar of fire by night to lead Israel on its wilderness journey. What are some ways God leads His people today?

NOTES

The Exodus Stage repeatedly shows the rebellion of God's people and the consequences that follow. This theme is seen throughout the entire Old Testament. Why?

The crossing of the Red Sea is one way God delivered His people in the Exodus Stage. What are some ways God delivers His people from trouble today?

Read *Hebrews 3:7-19*. How are God's people today different than the children of Israel in the wilderness? How are God's people today the same?

Find three events in Moses' life that show he was humble before God. Write the events and where you found them in the Bible in the spaces below.

1)

2)

3)

NOTES

CHAPTER FOUR
THE CONQUEST STAGE

1. Conquest Stage Overview

A. The Conquest Stage covers the time from 1405-1382 BC, and the book of Joshua.
   - This stage begins with the entry of Israel into the Promised Land, and ends with the death of Joshua.

B. The key people in the Conquest Stage are: Joshua, Caleb, Rahab and Achan.

C. The key events in the Conquest Stage are: Israel's invasion of the Promised Land (Palestine), Israel's conquering of the land, and Israel's division of the land.

D. The locations of the key events in this stage are:
   - Israel's invasion of the Promised Land: around the Jordan River.
   - Israel's conquering of the land: Canaan.
   - Israel's division of the land: for two and a half tribes, East Jordan; for nine and a half tribes, West Jordan.

E. There are other important events in this stage.
   - God parted the waters of the Jordan River so His people could enter the Promised Land (*Jos. 3:13-17*).
   - God caused the walls of Jericho to fall down (*Jos. 6:20*).
   - God caused the sun to stand still so Israel could win a battle (*Jos. 10:12-14*).

2. The Bible Account of the Conquest Stage

A. **Israel Invades the Promised Land** (*Jos. 1-5*; one month in 1405 B.C.)
   - As Israel prepared to invade the Promised Land, God promised Joshua He would be with him. With that promise from God, Joshua told Israel that they would enter the Promised Land in three days (*Jos. 1:1-9*).
   - Joshua sent two spies ahead to see what lay ahead in Jericho. The spies were discovered. A prostitute named Rahab, who had just come to faith in God, hid them in her home until they could escape (*Jos. 2:1-24*).
     ▶ Rahab is mentioned three times in the New Testament (*Mat. 1:5; Heb. 11:31; Jam. 2:25*). She was the great-great-grandmother of King David.[8]
   - Israel crossed the Jordan River with priests and the Ark of the Covenant leading the way. God told the priests to step out on the water as if it were solid rock. When they did, God parted the river and rolled back the waters. The entire nation of Israel crossed the Jordan on dry ground while the priests stood with the Ark in the middle of the Jordan River bed (*Jos. 3:1-17*).

NOTES

- ▶ As a memorial of the crossing, Israel placed twelve large stones on the western bank of the Jordan River. They also put another twelve in the middle of the river where the priests stood during the crossing (*Jos. 4:1-24*).
- Once Israel had completed the Jordan crossing and was on the western bank, Joshua ordered that all Israel's males be circumcised (*Jos. 5:2-9*).
  - ▶ The males who had come out of Egypt had been circumcised, but all of them except Joshua and Caleb had died in the wilderness.
  - ▶ None of the males born in the wilderness had been circumcised, which was a requirement to celebrate Passover.
- Four days after they crossed the Jordan River into the Promised Land, Israel also celebrated Passover according to God's instructions for the first time in many years (*Jos. 5:10*).
- The day after the Passover celebration, Israel began eating food from the Promised Land. God stopped His provision of manna that day because there was no longer need for it (*Jos. 5:11-12*).
- On the night before the battle of Jericho, the Commander of the Army of the Lord (probably the Son of God) visited Joshua. Joshua is told that Israel will defeat Jericho (*Jos. 5:13-15*).
  - ▶ The Commander also told Joshua to take off his shoes, for he was standing on holy ground (see *Exo. 3:5*).

B. **Israel Conquers the Promised Land** (*Jos. 6-12*; about 1405-1398 BC).
- The Central Campaign began with the battle of Jericho. Here, Joshua led Israel in daily marches around the city for six days. On the seventh day the priests blew trumpets, the people shouted and the city's walls were miraculously destroyed. The army of Israel destroyed all of Jericho except Rahab and her household (*Jos. 6*).
- After a great victory at Jericho, Israel sent a small army to fight a small city called Ai. Much to Joshua's surprise, Ai defeated Israel and killed many Israeli soldiers (*Jos. 7*).
  - ▶ God told Joshua that Israel's defeat at Ai was due to sin in Israel. Someone had taken cursed things from Jericho. Achan, from the tribe of Judah, soon confessed to the crime and was executed.
- At God's command, Joshua took 30,000 men to capture Ai. This time Israel won, and destroyed Ai completely (*Jos. 8:1-29*).
- Joshua renewed Israel's covenant with God. He read the blessings and curses of the Law of Moses from Mt. Gerizim and Mt. Ebal (*Jos. 8:30-35*).
- The Southern Campaign began with word spreading about Israel's victories at Jericho and Ai. This caused a delegation from Gibeon to approach Israel, pretending that they were from a far-off city (*Jos. 9*).
  - ▶ Actually, Gibeon was only about five miles from Ai.
  - ▶ They wanted a treaty with Israel, but knew that the Law would prevent Israel from having a treaty with a nearby Canaanite city.
  - ▶ Gibeon tricked Israel into a treaty.
  - ▶ When Israel discovered Gibeon had tricked them, they cursed Gibeon.
  - ▶ Joshua ordered that Gibeon become slaves for the house of God.
- When the King of Jerusalem found out about Gibeon's treaty with Israel, he agreed with four other kings to destroy Gibeon and Israel (*Jos. 10*).

- Joshua attacked the kings' alliance before they could attack Israel.
- God sent a hailstorm and extended daylight to help Joshua defeat the kings.
- Joshua's men tracked the kings to a cave in Makkedah. There, Israel captured and executed the five kings.
- God then commanded Joshua to complete the Southern Campaign. Israel fought and won a series of battles to take the land there.
- The Northern Campaign brought a group of kings together to fight Israel. They camped by the waters of Merom. God told Joshua to cut the legs of the kings' horses so they could not run. He also instructed Joshua to burn the chariots of the kings' army. Joshua obeyed. The Israelites not only won the battle at Merom, but also easily flattened the cities in the northern part of the Promised Land (*Jos. 11*).

C. **Israel Divides the Promised Land** (*Jos. 14-24*; about 1398-1390 BC).
- Israel divided the Promised Land between the tribes as follows (*Jos. 15-21*).
    - The land west of the Jordan was divided between nine-and-a-half tribes.
        - One-half tribe of Manasseh.
        - Ephraim.
        - Judah.
        - Benjamin.
        - Simeon.
        - Zebulun.
        - Issachar.
        - Asher.
        - Naphtali.
        - Dan.
    - The land east of the Jordan was divided between two-and-a-half tribes.
        - Reuben.
        - Gad.
        - One-half tribe of Manasseh.
    - No land was given to Levi. God Himself was their portion. But Levi would receive 48 special cities from the eleven tribes.
    - Caleb received Hebron as a reward for fully following God (*Jos. 14:7-12*).
- The tabernacle was set up in the Promised Land (Palestine) at Shiloh. The two-and-a-half tribes east of the Jordan set up an altar to remind them that they had a common bond with the tribes west of the Jordan (*Jos. 22*).
    - The tribes of the west misunderstood the altar set up by the tribes of the east. They thought the altar was a sign of rebellion against Israel and the tabernacle.
    - The tribes of the west threatened to attack the tribes of the east.
    - The issue was settled after Phinehas, Aaron's grandson, led a group from the western tribes to look into the meaning of the altar.
    - The altar was a witness that the Lord is God (*Jos.22:34*).
        - In the same way, Jesus told His disciples that their love for each other would be a witness that pointed people to Christ (*Joh. 13:35*).

- Joshua called Israel together and delivered his last words to them (*Jos. 23-24*).
    ▶ He reminded Israel that God had been faithful, so they needed to obey His covenant.
    ▶ He went over the history of God's goodness, and told Israel to serve God.

NOTES

Questions:

As you consider how to preach from the events in the Conquest Stage, think about how God did all that was necessary to keep His people safe. Just as He had parted the Red Sea to help Israel escape from Egypt's army, God parted the Jordan River to give His people safe passage into the Promised Land. He caused the sun to stand still so Joshua's army would be victorious over its enemies.

Think about your life. What are some of the things God has done to show He cares for you?

List five things in the Conquest Stage that show God was faithful in his promise to deliver the Promised Land to Israel. Write where you found these things in the Bible, too.

1)

2)

3)

4)

5)

Chapter Five
The Judges Stage

1. Judges Stage Overview

A. The Judges Stage covers the time from 1382-1043 BC, and the books of Judges, Ruth, and 1 Samuel 1-7.
  - This stage begins with the death of Joshua, and ends with the judgeship of Samuel.

B. The key people in the Judges Stage are: Ehud, Barak, Deborah, Gideon, Jephthah, Samson, Ruth, Naomi, Boaz, Hannah, Eli, and Samuel.

C. The key events in the Judges Stage are: the ministry of the 15 judges, the marriage of Ruth to Boaz, the prayer of Hannah, and the death of Eli.

D. The locations of the key events in this stage are:
  - The ministry of the 15 judges: Canaan.
  - The marriage of Ruth to Boaz: Bethlehem.
  - The prayer of Hannah: Shiloh.
  - The death of Eli: Shiloh.

E. There are other important things about this stage.
  - The Judges Stage is the time of the greatest spiritual darkness in Israel.
  - The story of Samson, the Nazarite strongman (*Jud. 13:1-16:31*).
  - The capture of the Ark of the Covenant (*1 Sam. 4:10-11*).
  - Ruth the Moabite woman becomes part of David and Jesus' family line (*Rut. 4:13-22; Mat. 1:5-16*).

F. Even though the Judges are far from perfect leaders, Samson, Gideon, Barak, Jephthah and Samuel are mentioned in *Hebrews 11:32* as men of great faith in God.

G. H.L. Willmington compares the Conquest Stage and the Judges Stage by contrasting the books of Joshua and Judges[9]:

Joshua and Judges Contrasted

Book of Joshua	Book of Judges
Victory	Defeat
Freedom	Slavery
Faith	Unbelief
Progress	Decline
Obedience	Disobedience
Heavenly Vision	Earthly Emphasis
Joy	Sorrow
Strength	Weakness
Unity	Disunity
Strong Leader	No Leader

2. The Bible Account of the Judges Stage

A. **Twelve Military Reformers** (*Judges 1-16*; times of the judges overlap to total about 300 years before the judgeships of Eli and Samuel).
- The Judges Stage is a time when Israel often forgot their need to follow God. The Bible says it was a time when people did what they thought was right, without caring about God or other people (*17:26*).
- The Judges Stage has a series of stories that follow a similar pattern.
    - ▶ Israel sins against God.
    - ▶ As a result, Israel is oppressed by another nation.
    - ▶ Then Israel cries out to God for help.
    - ▶ God saves Israel through the leadership of a judge.
        - ▷ A "judge" here is a military reformer, not a legal expert.
- Mesopotamia had oppressed Israel for eight years. The judge Othniel defeated Mesopotamia and led Israel into 40 years of peace (*1:12-13; 3:8-11*).
    - ▶ Othniel was both the son-in-law and nephew of Caleb.
    - ▶ Othniel captured a strong Canaanite city.
- When Moab had afflicted Israel for 18 years, Ehud was God's answer. He killed Eglon, the Moabite king, and led Israel into 80 years of peace (*3:12-30*).
    - ▶ Ehud also organized an army for Israel that killed 10,000 enemy soldiers.
- The judge Shamgar brought relief to Israel when they had been dominated by Philistia. He killed 600 Philistines with a pointed rod called an "oxgoad" (*3:31*).
- The Canaanites afflicted Israel for 20 years. The judge Barak defeated the Canaanites and led Israel into 40 years of peace (*4-5*).
    - ▶ The judge Deborah encouraged Barak to raise an army of 10,000.
    - ▶ Barak defeated the Canaanite king Sisera at the base of Mt. Tabor.
        - ▷ Sisera was later killed by a woman named Jael.
    - ▶ Barak and Deborah sang a praise song to God for Israel's victory over Canaan.
- Midian had burdened Israel for seven years when God called the judge Gideon to rescue Israel (*6-8*).
    - ▶ Gideon prepared for the task by destroying his family idols.
    - ▶ He raised an army of 10,000 men, which God reduced to 300 before the battle.
    - ▶ Gideon's army of 300 defeated 135,000 Midianite soldiers.
    - ▶ Gideon's victory led to 40 years of peace in Israel. However, Gideon made a golden vest which became an idol to Israel.
- Not much is known about the judge Tola. We do know that he led Israel into 23 years of peace (*10:1*).
- The judge Jair and his 30 sons rescued 30 cities in Israel from foreign domination. Jair led Israel into another 23 years of peace (*10:3-5*).
- Jephthah's time as judge was good for Israel, but tragic for him (*10:6-12:17*).
    - ▶ Ammon had burdened Israel for 18 years. When Jephthah defeated Ammon, he led Israel into six years of peace.
    - ▶ The night before the battle Jephthah made a careless vow. He said

if Israel was victorious over Ammon that he would sacrifice the first thing that greeted him. His daughter met him first. Jephthah sadly went through with the sacrifice.
- The judge Ibzan led Israel into seven years of peace (*12:8-10*).
- The judge Elon led Israel into ten years of peace (*12:11-12*).
- Abdon led Israel into eight years of peace (*12:13-15*).
- The most famous judge might be Samson. He led Israel into 20 years of peace after 40 years of affliction under Philistia (*13-16*).
  - ▶ Samson was raised as a Nazarite. According to his vow, he could not cut his hair, touch a dead body, or take strong drink.
    - ▷ Samson's mother was visited by the angel of the Lord who told her of Samson's future birth (*13:2-3*). There are three other women in the Bible who received pre-birth promises from angels:
      - ◆ Sarah (*Gen. 18:10-14*).
      - ◆ Elisabeth (*Luk. 1:13*).
      - ◆ Mary (*Luk. 1:30*).
  - ▶ A man of great strength, Samson:
    - ▷ Killed a lion on the way to his wedding.
    - ▷ Killed 30 Philistines to pay off a clothing debt.
    - ▷ Killed 1,000 Philistines with the jawbone of a donkey.
    - ▷ Ripped off an iron gate at Gaza.
  - ▶ Samson was tricked by Delilah who gave him over to the Philistines.
    - ▷ The Philistines shaved, blinded, and enslaved Samson.
  - ▶ God empowered Samson to pull down a Philistine temple. When Samson destroyed the temple, Samson was killed along with many Philistines.
- Three men in the time of these judges were known for their evil.
  - ▶ Abimelech was the son of Gideon. He arranged for the murder of 69 of his half-brothers. God killed him through an evil spirit and an old woman (*Jud. 9*).
  - ▶ Micah was a thief and an idol worshiper. He was encouraged by his mother to start his own religion. He hired an unfaithful priest to lead his family and others in worshiping his idol. The priest became the private priest of the tribe of Dan, who also practiced idolatry (*Jud. 17-18*).
  - ▶ There was a Levite who traveled to the land of Benjamin with his concubine. He saved himself by allowing a crowd of sex perverts to violate and murder her.
    - ▷ He then cut her body into twelve pieces and sent a piece to each tribe in Israel.
    - ▷ An army of 450,000 was raised to punish the men who killed her.
    - ▷ Benjamin tribe leaders refused to hand over the men to justice.
    - ▷ A civil war occurs and leaves only 600 Benjamite soldiers alive.
    - ▷ A plan is worked out to provide wives for the 600 Benjamite soldiers so the tribe of Benjamin would not disappear.

B. **Ruth** (*Ruth 1-4*; around 1100 BC)
- In a time when Israel was faithless to God, Ruth the Moabitess showed faith in God. As she continued in faith, she became part of the family line of David and Jesus.

- During a famine, Elimelech, his wife Naoming and their two sons moved from Bethlehem to Moab (*Rut. 1*).
  - The sons married Moabite women.
  - Soon after, the sons and their father died.
  - Naomi returned to Bethlehem with her daughter-in-law Ruth, who had given up her Moabite gods for the God of Israel.
- In Bethlehem, Ruth worked in the wheat field of Boaz, a close relative of Elimelech (*Rut. 2*).
  - Boaz fell in love with Ruth at their first meeting.
  - Naomi began planning for their wedding when she heard about Ruth and Boaz.
- Naomi sent Ruth to Boaz to request that Boaz fulfill his role as a kinsman redeemer (*Rut. 3*).
  - The kinsman redeemer was the defender of a family's rights. He was a close relative to someone who was poor, and had the resources to buy that relative out of slavery, or to buy back ancestral land.
    - Boaz would fulfill not only the land-redeeming duty of a kinsman redeemer, but also the duty of providing an heir for Mahlon, Ruth's deceased husband. He did this by marrying Ruth and having a son with her.[10]
  - Boaz was happy with Ruth's request. Yet he had to offer the role of kinsman redeemer to a relative closer than he.
  - Ruth returned home and trusted God for results.
- Boaz arranged a meeting with the kinsman redeemer who was closer than he was (*Rut. 4*).
  - The closer kinsman redeemer agreed to allow Boaz to fulfill the role of kinsman redeemer, including marrying Ruth.
  - Ruth and Boaz had a baby boy, Obed, who became the grandfather of David.

C. **Hannah, Eli and Samuel** (*1 Samuel 1-7*; about 1100-1050 BC).
- The story of the judges Eli and Samuel begin with the story of Samuel's mother Hannah. Samuel would become the last judge of Israel. He was also the prophet God used to help Israel change from a government of judges to a government led by a king.
- People treated Hannah with scorn because she could not have children. But Hannah was a woman of prayer. As she prayed at Shiloh, Hannah promised God that any son she had would be raised as a Nazarite. Through the high priest Eli, God told Hannah that He had heard her prayer (*1 Sam. 1:1-19*).
- Hannah gives birth to a son, Samuel. In gratitude and according to her promise she brings Samuel to Eli to serve at Shiloh (*1 Sam. 1: 20-2:11, 18-21*).
  - She praises God through a song. The song thanks God for blessing the poor and humble and judging the earth with justice.
    - The song also has a prophecy about the Messiah (*1 Sam. 2:10*).
  - Hannah later has three more sons and two daughters.
- Eli had great respect and responsibility as the high priest. But the behavior of his sons showed that Eli was not a good father (*1 Sam. 2-4*).

NOTES

- ▶ Eli's sons worshiped Belial as their god. They stole offerings meant for the God of Israel, and mistreated His people.
- ▶ Eli's sons committed adultery in the tabernacle.
- ▶ They caused God's people to follow them in sin.
- ▶ God warned Eli's sons to repent through both an unnamed prophet and Samuel.
* Eli's sons were killed when the Philistines defeated Israel and captured the Ark of the Covenant. Eli fell out of his chair when he heard of his sons' deaths. The fall broke Eli's neck and he died.
* The Ark of the Covenant caused a lot of trouble for the Philistines. God punished them for stealing the Ark, and for not handling it in the right way (*1 Sam. 5-7*).
    - ▶ At Ashdod the Ark destroyed the statue of the Philistine god Dagon, and caused boils on the people there.
    - ▶ At Gath the Ark brought destruction and more boils.
    - ▶ At Ekron the Ark brought fear and more boils.
    - ▶ At Beth-shemesh, a town in Israel, the Ark first brought great joy. But God sent a plague of punishment on the town when people looked into the Ark.
    - ▶ The Ark was next taken to Kirjath-Jearim, where it remained until David took it to Jerusalem.
* The prophet Samuel was the last and perhaps greatest judge of Israel. Each year, Samuel would travel to Shiloh, Bethel, Gilgal and Mizpah. He then returned to his hometown Ramah to judge Israel. At Ramah, Samuel built an altar to God (*1 Sam. 7:15-17*).
    - ▶ God revealed Himself to Samuel as a boy when he was serving at Shiloh (*1 Sam. 3:19-21*).
    - ▶ Samuel led Israel into revival and the destruction of the Philistines (*1 Sam. 7:3-14*).
    - ▶ As stated earlier, Samuel led Israel through the change from the time of judges into the time of kings.

Questions:

Look through the Judges Stage. Find three people who stayed true to God in this stage. Write down how they were true to God, and the place in the Bible where you can find it.

1)

2)

3)

Compare Hannah's song in *1 Sam. 2:1-10* with the song of Mary in *Luke 1:46-55*. What is alike in the two songs? What is different?

The Bible says the Judges Stage was a time when "everyone did what was right in his own eyes." What is the problem with living like that? Give some examples of how life is like that today.

Why do you think God punished the Philistines for handling the Ark of the Covenant in the wrong way? Use Scripture to support your answer.

Chapter Six
The United Kingdom Stage

1. United Kingdom Stage Overview

A. The United Kingdom Stage covers the time from about 1043-931 BC, covering: 1 Samuel 8-31, 2 Samuel, 1 Kings 1-11, 1 Chronicles, 2 Chronicles 1-9, Psalms, Proverbs, Ecclesiastes, and Song of Solomon.
- This stage begins with Saul becoming king of Israel, and ends with the death of Solomon.

B. The key people in the United Kingdom Stage are: the kings Saul, David, and Solomon. Each king ruled for 40 years in this stage.

C. The key events in the United Kingdom Stage are: the anointing of David as king, David's capture of Jerusalem, the bringing of the Ark of the Covenant into Jerusalem, God's covenant with David, and the construction of the first temple.

D. The locations of the key events in this stage are:
- The three times David is anointed king: Bethlehem (by the prophet Samuel), Hebron (by two tribes), and Hebron again (by all twelve tribes).
- David's capture of Jerusalem: Jerusalem.
- The bringing of the Ark into Jerusalem: the route from Kirjath-Jearim into Jerusalem.
- God's covenant with David: Jerusalem.
- The construction of the first temple: Jerusalem.

E. There are other important things in this stage.
- The musical talent and wisdom of David and Solomon is used by God to produce many of the songs and sayings of this stage (Psalms, Proverbs, Ecclesiastes, and Song of Solomon).
  - ▶ These books of the Bible are known as "Wisdom Literature." They use literary forms that set them apart from other books of the Bible. The Psalms are poems and songs. Proverbs is a collection of short sayings. Ecclesiastes is a book of advice and perspective. Song of Solomon is a collection of poems sung between lovers in a marriage relationship. Each "wisdom book" has something to say about how people can live a better life by following God's ways.
- Saul, the first king of Israel, completely violates the Law of Moses by trying to reach the dead prophet Samuel through the witch of En Dor (*1 Sam. 28*).
- David commits adultery with a woman named Bathsheba, and uses murder to try and hide his sin. Yet, when God confronts him through the prophet Nathan, David repents and takes responsibility for his actions (*2 Sam. 12*).
- Israel becomes an international power during the reign of Solomon (*1 Kin. 4:34; 10:1-15*).

2. The Bible Account of the United Kingdom Stage

NOTES

A. **Saul: His Rise and Fall** (*1 Sam. 8-31*; about 1050-1010 BC).
   - The prophet and judge Samuel was getting old. His sons were wicked, and not fit to lead.
     - ▶ Israel also wanted to be more like all the other nations.
     - ▶ Despite Samuel's warnings that a king would rule over them in ways they would not like, Israel demanded that they have a king.
     - ▶ God told Samuel to give them a king (*1 Sam. 8*).
   - At God's command, Samuel chose Saul to be Israel's first king (*1 Sam. 9*).
     - ▶ Saul went to Samuel seeking help to find some lost animals.
     - ▶ God had told Samuel that Saul was coming.
     - ▶ When they met, Samuel told Saul about God's plans.
     - ▶ The Lord told Samuel that he should anoint Saul as the commander of Israel.
   - Samuel anointed Saul at Ramah. Samuel then arranged for the twelve tribes of Israel to present themselves to Saul at Mizpah, where Israel proclaimed Saul as their king (*1 Sam. 10*).
     - ▶ At first Saul was a humble leader. (Pay attention to Saul's behavior from the time he was anointed to the end of his life).
   - Saul showed his ability to lead by raising and leading an army to free the city of Jabesh-Gilead from the Ammonites. Israel is very successful in this effort, and celebrated that Saul was their king. Samuel told Saul to always serve God (*1 Sam. 11-12*).
   - Saul was not wise. In preparing to battle the Philistines, he chose not to wait for a priest to present a burnt offering to the Lord. Instead, Saul took on the role of the priest himself. This offense caused God to withdraw His blessing on Saul as king of Israel (*1 Sam. 13*).
     - ▶ Saul's lack of judgment was shown more often as his reign continued.
       - ▷ He ordered a fast that put his own son's life in danger (*1 Sam. 14*).
       - ▷ Instead of completely destroying the Amalekites as God had ordered, Saul spared the fine livestock and the Amalekite king Agag. As a result, Samuel rejected Saul as Israel's king (*1 Sam. 15*).
         - ✦ This event led to the total rejection of Saul by God. It teaches the important truth that it is better to obey than to sacrifice for sins. When we obey God the first time, a sacrifice is not needed (*Eph. 6:13*).
       - ▷ Saul became possessed by an evil spirit (*1 Sam. 16:14, 18:10, 19:9*).
       - ▷ Saul tried to kill David (*1 Sam. 18:11, 21, 25, 19:1, 10, 15*),
       - ▷ Saul cursed and tried to kill his own son Jonathan (*1 Sam. 20:30-33*).
       - ▷ Saul slaughtered 85 priests of God in the city of Nob (*1 Sam. 22:17-19*).
       - ▷ Saul broke the Law of Moses again by seeking to contact the dead prophet Samuel through a witch at En Dor (*1 Sam. 28*).
   - Saul and his sons were killed in battle against the Philistines on Mt. Gilboa (*1 Sam. 31*).

NOTES

Questions:

What do you think caused the changes in Saul from a humble leader to a selfish king? Give Bible verses that support your answer.

What would you preach to tell people today how to avoid Saul's downfall in their own lives? Use Scripture to support your answers.

- B. **David's Reign** (*1 Sam. 16-2 Sam. 24; 1 Chr. 11-29; 1 Kin. 2*. David's reign was from about 1010-970 BC).
  - David grew up as a shepherd boy near the city of Bethlehem. The prophet Samuel followed God's leading to anoint David as king of Israel. God reminded Samuel that even though David was not the biggest or most handsome in his family, God was looking at David's heart rather than his outside features (*1 Sam. 16:7*). When David was anointed, the Spirit of God came upon him (*1 Sam. 16:1-13*).
  - David was also a skilled poet and musician. When Saul was troubled by an evil spirit, David's music comforted the king (*1 Sam. 16:14-23*).
  - David became a hero in Israel when he defeated the giant Philistine warrior Goliath. David used weapons he had used as a shepherd (a sling and some stones), instead of the usual military weapons from that time (*1 Sam. 17:1-58*).
  - David's fame grew quickly. Saul became very jealous, and attempted to kill David both privately and by openly hunting him (*1 Sam. 18:11, 21, 25; 23:15-26*).
  - David also made connections with Saul's family. He began a deep and lifelong friendship with Saul's son Jonathan (*1 Sam. 18:1-4*). He was made chief commander of Saul's armies (*1 Sam. 18:5*). David also married Saul's daughter Michal, the first of his many wives (*1 Sam. 18:27*).
  - Saul's jealousy led him to hunt for David. David kept moving to stay out of Saul's reach.
    - ▶ David ran to the city of Nob, where he lied to the high priest in order to avoid questions about Saul. (*1 Sam. 21:1-9*).
    - ▶ He then went to the city of Gath in Philistia and pretended to be insane to avoid capture by Achish, the king of Gath (*1 Sam. 21:10-15*).
    - ▶ David began gathering a group of men who were unhappy with Saul as king (*1 Sam. 22:1-2; 23:13*). They went to Moab to stay away from Saul, but God told David to go on to Judah (*1 Sam. 22:3-5*).
    - ▶ David had the opportunity to kill Saul twice. Yet, since Saul was God's anointed, David refused to harm him (*1 Sam. 24:1-15; 26:1-16*).

- ▶ David married his second wife, a widow named Abigail (*1 Sam. 25:1-42*).
- ▶ David put an end to Saul's hunt for him by staying with the Philistines. Although Achish the king of Gath expected David to fight in battle against Saul, the other Philistine leaders told David to stay away from the fight (*1 Sam. 27, 29*).
  - ▷ Saul and his sons, including Jonathan, were in the battle with the Philistines (*1 Sam. 31:1-7*).
- When Saul died, God told David to go to Hebron. There, the men of Judah anointed David as their king (*2 Sam. 1-4*). This was David's second anointing.
- After a seven-year war, David defeated the house of Saul and was anointed at Hebron as king by all twelve tribes of Israel (*2 Sam. 3-5*). This was David's third anointing.
- After his third and final anointing, David captured Jerusalem and made it his capital (*2 Sam. 5:6-10*).
  - ▶ David then brought the Ark of the Covenant into Jerusalem (*2 Sam. 6:1-19; 1 Chr. 13:1-14, 15:1-16:43*). In review we see that:
    - ▷ God commanded Moses to make the ark (*Exo. 25:10-22*).[11]
    - ▷ The ark traveled through the forty-year wilderness journey with the rest of the tabernacle.
    - ▷ The ark was eventually set up in Shiloh, the first Israelite capital (*Jos. 18:1*).
    - ▷ The ark was carried into battle, where the Philistines captured it (*1 Sam. 4:11*).
    - ▷ The Philistines passed the ark around their cities because it brought them trouble (*1 Sam. 5*).
    - ▷ The ark caused a plague in the Philistine city of Beth-shemesh, where the men had looked inside of it (*1 Sam. 6:19*).
    - ▷ The Philistines returned the ark to Israel at the city of Kirath Jearim, where it stayed for twenty years until David brought it to Jerusalem (*1 Sam.7:1-2*).
  - ▶ David wanted to build a temple for God. However, God did not allow David to do so (*2 Sam. 7:17; 1 Chr. 17:4*).
- God made a covenant with David (*2 Sam. 7:8-17; 1 Chr. 17:7-15*) that changed history. The promises in this covenant say:
  - ▶ David would have a child who will succeed him and establish his kingdom.
  - ▶ This son (Solomon), would build God's temple instead of David.
  - ▶ The throne of his kingdom would be established forever.
  - ▶ The throne would not be taken away from him even though his sins may deserve it.
  - ▶ David's house, throne, and kingdom would be established forever (*Luk. 1:28-33, 68-75; Act. 15:13-18*).
- David's heart was shown in his kindness as king. He sought out his friend Jonathan's lame son, Mephibosheth, to make sure he had food and shelter (*2 Sam. 9:6-8*).
- David committed adultery with Bathsheba. To hide their sin, David arranged to have her husband Uriah killed during a battle (*2 Sam. 11*).
  - ▶ Nathan the prophet confronted David. David confessed his sin

NOTES

(*2 Sam. 12:1-12; Ps. 32, 51*).
- ▶ God forgave David. Yet there were still consequences for David's sin.
  - ▷ His infant son with Bathsheba would die (*2 Sam. 12:13*).
  - ▷ Amnon, his son, would rape his half-sister (and David's daughter) Tamar (*2 Sam. 13:14*).
  - ▷ David's son Absalom would murder Amnon (*2 Sam. 13:29*).
  - ▷ Absalom would lead a rebellion against David (*2 Sam. 15-18*).
- In the middle of a three-year plague in Israel, God told David that the reason for the plague was due to the cruelty of Saul's house toward Gibeon (*2 Sam. 21:1-14*).
  - ▶ Israel had made a covenant in Joshua's time that these Gibeonites would not be harmed (*Joshua 9*).
  - ▶ David talked with the Gibeonite leaders. Together they agreed to execute seven of Saul's sons who had probably been involved in the cruelty toward Gibeon. After the execution, the plague ended.
- Satan tempted David to number the people of Israel. David gave in to his pride by wanting to know how large his kingdom was. God responds with a plague that is only stopped when David asked the death angel to stop it (*2 Sam. 24; 1 Chr. 21*).
- At this point, David is nearly 70 years old. He led a service to dedicate the future temple. He gave great amounts of wealth for the temple, and raised more money from others (*1 Chr. 22-29*).
  - ▶ David gave Solomon the plans for the temple that he had received from God.
  - ▶ David then said a powerful prayer to honor God.
- David also wrote about half the psalms we have in the book of Psalms (*2 Sam. 22:1; 23:1-3*).
  - ▶ The Psalms were very important writings during the United Kingdom stage. They were used in public and private worship. They have proven to be timeless expressions of praise, repentance, worship and thanksgiving for God's people from the time of David to today.
  - ▶ David and others wrote psalms that fall into several areas.
- <u>Psalms of Repentance</u>: *6, 32, 38, 51, 102, 130, 143*.
  - ▶ Psalms of repentance resulted when an individual recognized the consequences of personal sin. In the Psalms, David wrote five of the seven psalms of repentance.
  - ▶ *Psalm 51* may be the most famous psalm of repentance. David wrote the psalm as he repented of his sins of adultery with Bathsheba, and the murder of Uriah.
    - ▷ David begins by taking full responsibility for his sin. He does not blame anyone else. The fault is David's alone (*51:1-3*):

Have mercy upon me, O God, According to Your loving-kindness; According to the multitude of Your tender mercies, Blot out my transgressions. Wash me thoroughly from my iniquity, and cleanse me from my sin. For I acknowledge my transgressions and my sin is always before me.

- ▷ Forgiveness follows only when a sinner acknowledges his sin (*1 Joh. 1:8-10*).

▷ David says his sin against God was so serious, it was as though he had sinned against no one else (*51:4*):

Against You, You only, have I sinned, and done this evil in Your sight - That You may be found just when You speak, and blameless when You judge.

▷ Paul quotes the last part of this verse in *Romans 3:4* to show that all are guilty of sin before God.
▷ David asks to be cleansed of his sin with hyssop (*Lev. 14:4; Num. 19:6*).
  • This is a ritual act of cleansing from sin.
▷ David also asks to be washed clean from sin "as white as snow" (*Isa. 1:18*), and that God would blot out his iniquities (*Psa. 51:7, 9*):

Purge me with hyssop, and I shall be clean; Wash me and I shall be whiter than snow…Hide Your face from my sins, and blot out all my iniquities.

  • David is seen repeatedly asking to be made clean. This shows how deeply David felt the sting of his sin.
  • Through His blood, Jesus purged the sins of believers everywhere (*Heb. 1:3*).
▷ David recognizes that God alone can restore him. He asks God to create a clean heart within him (*Psa. 51:10*).
  • The word "create" here is the same word used in *Genesis 1:1*.
  • Creating a clean heart and creating the universe are things God alone can do.
▷ David asks God to restore the joy of his salvation (*Psa. 51:12*).
  • This is another way of David stating his desire to return to fellowship with God, his first love.
  • Later, Christ commanded the church at Ephesus to return to their first love (*Rev. 2:4-5*).
▷ David shows that he completely depends on God's mercy and grace for forgiveness rather than offerings and sacrifices (*Psa. 51:16-17*):

For You do not desire sacrifice, or else I would give it; You do not delight in burnt offering. The sacrifices of God are a broken spirit, A broken and a contrite heart—These, O God, You will not despise.

  • There was no sacrifice for the sin of adultery. Someone guilty of adultery was to be stoned to death (*Lev. 20:10*). David trusted in God's mercy and grace. There was no other way for him to escape the penalty he deserved.
  • A sacrifice meant nothing without repentance (*Isa. 1:12-20*).
  • This psalm showed that the real path to restoration is through repentance from the heart of the sinner.

NOTES

- <u>Psalms asking for God's judgment</u>: *35, 55, 58, 59, 69, 83, 109, 137, 140.*
  - ▶ Sometimes a writer of a psalm asked God to bring harm to his enemies. Some examples include asking God to:
    - ▷ Fight against them (*35:1*).
    - ▷ Confuse them (*35:4*).
    - ▷ Scatter them (*35:5*).
    - ▷ Allow death to capture them (*55:15*).
    - ▷ Send them to hell (*55:15*).
    - ▷ Break their teeth (*58:8*).
    - ▷ Withhold mercy from them (*59:5*).
    - ▷ Give them over to Satan (*109:6*).
    - ▷ Let their days be few (*109:8*).
  - ▶ This may seem to conflict with Jesus' instruction to bless our enemies (*Mat. 5:44*). Yet judgment on evil and evildoers is also part of the New Testament (*Mat.18:6; 23:33; 26:24; Gal. 1:8-9; 5:12; Jam. 5:3; Jude 13, 15; 2 Pet. 2:12, 22; 2 The. 2:10-12; Rev. 14:10-11*).
    - ▷ Many of the psalms against evildoers come from sympathy for persecuted and injured people.
    - ▷ Some of these psalms are asking for success on the battlefield (*Ps. 144:5-7*). These often refer to wars God has approved.
    - ▷ Many of these psalms are talking about the final judgment facing the wicked.
    - ▷ Even in these psalms, God extends grace to the wicked if they will listen to His warnings and repent. So there is no excuse for the wicked.
- <u>Psalms of Devotion</u>: *4, 9, 12, 13, 14, 16, 17, 18, 19, 22, 23, 24, 27, 30, 31, 33, 34, 35, 37, 40, 42, 43, 46, 50, 55, 56, 61, 62, 63, 66, 68, 69, 71, 73, 75, 76, 77, 80, 81, 84, 85, 88, 90, 91, 95, 100, 103, 106, 107, 111, 115, 116, 118, 119, 122, 123, 126, 133, 136, 138, 139, 141, 142, 144, 147, 148, 149, 150.*
  - ▶ Psalms of devotion are the most common type of psalm. These psalms have promises from God to the believer. The psalms are written from many different life circumstances. They show God is faithful when His people are sad or happy, living in wealth or poverty, in persecution or celebration.
  - ▶ The most famous psalm in the Bible is usually said to be *Psalm 23*. It is also the most famous confession of faith in the Old Testament. It is a wonderful example of a psalm of devotion:

> *The LORD is my shepherd; I shall not want. He makes me to lie down in green pastures; He leads me beside the still waters. He restores my soul; He leads me in the paths of righteousness, For His name's sake. Yea, though I walk through the valley of the shadow of death, I will fear no evil; For You are with me; Your rod and Your staff, they comfort me. You prepare a table before me in the presence of my enemies; You anoint my head with oil; My cup runs over. Surely goodness and mercy shall follow me all the days of my life; And I will dwell in the house of the LORD Forever.*

▷ David says that the Lord is his Shepherd. See *John 10:1-18*.[12] Because of this, David has everything he needs (*23:1*).
   ◆ The Shepherd provides green pastures to refresh his soul (*23:2*).
   ◆ The Shepherd provides still waters when he is thirsty and weary (*23:2*).
   ◆ The Shepherd restores him when he needs revival (*23:3*).
   ◆ The Shepherd leads him on the right paths when he needs guidance (*23:3*).
   ◆ The Shepherd walks with him when death confronts him (*23:4*).
   ◆ The Shepherd provides him a feasting table of victory when his enemies confront him (*23:5*).
   ◆ The Shepherd anoints his head with oil when his soul is wounded (*23:5*).
   ◆ The Shepherd fills his life with goodness and mercy (*23:6*).
   ◆ The Shepherd provides a permanent and eternal dwelling for him (*23:6*).
   ◆ This psalm, along with many others, has brought great comfort and courage to believers for many generations.
- Historical Psalms: *78, 105, 106*.
   ▶ These three psalms cover the history of Israel. They contrast the sins of Israel with the grace of God, as in the chart that follows:

Historical Psalms: The Sins of Israel and the Grace of God[13]

Israel's Sins	God's Grace
Refused to walk in God's law (*78:10*)	Remembered His covenant when Israel cried to Him (*105:8-11*)
Forgot God's works (*78:11, 42; 106:13*)	Divided the sea (*78:13*)
Spoke against God (*78:19*)	Led them with a cloud by day and a fire by night (*78:14*)
Didn't trust God's salvation (*78:22*)	Provided water out of rocks (*78:15*)
Lied to God (*78:36*)	Provided manna for them (*78:24*)
Grieved God (*78:40*)	Compassionate and forgiving (*78:38*)
Limited God (*78:41*)	Gave signs for them in Egypt (*78:43; 105:27-36*)
Worshiped idols (*78:58; 106:19*)	Brought them to the border of the Promised Land (*78:54*)
Envied God's chosen leader Moses (*106:16*)	Cast out their enemies before them (*78:55*)
Despised the Promised Land (*106:24*)	Chose David to lead them (*78:70-71*)
Complained in their tents (*106:25*)	Allowed no man to hurt them (*105:14*)
Ate the sacrifices of the dead (*106:28*)	Fed them (*78:72*)
Mingled with those who didn't worship God (*106:35*)	Corrected kings for their sake (*105:14*)
Sacrificed their children to devils (*106:37*)	Elevated them through Joseph (*105:17*)
Shed innocent blood (*106:38*)	Gave them all the riches of Egypt (*105:37*)

NOTES

- Psalms of Ascent: *120-134*.
  - ▶ Many scholars believe these fifteen psalms are in the Bible thanks to King Hezekiah, who is the author of 10 of them (*120, 121, 123, 125, 126, 128, 129, 130, 132, 134*).
    - ▷ *Psalm 121* especially shows Hezekiah's trust and thanks.
      - ✦ Hezekiah wrote his psalms out of gratitude to God, Who had healed him of a fatal disease. After he recovered Hezekiah said he would sing his songs of thanksgiving to God, with the stringed instruments, for the rest of his life in God's house (*Isa. 38:20*).
      - ✦ He then added five more psalms from David (*122, 124, 131, 133*), and Solomon (*127*) to bring the total number of the psalms of ascent to fifteen. One for every year of additional life God had promised him (*2 Kin. 21:6*).
      - ✦ Jewish tradition said that these songs were sung as the choir climbed the stairs leading up to the court of men at the Temple.
      - ✦ These psalms come from hearts full of thanks. Each psalm of ascent says something about the goodness of God and His blessings to His people.
- Acrostic Psalms: *9, 10, 25, 34, 37, 111, 112, 119, 145*.
  - ▶ Acrostic psalms were arranged so each line of the psalm began, in alphabetical order, with a Hebrew letter.
    - ▷ This acrostic arrangement helped people memorize these psalms.
  - ▶ Not every acrostic psalm uses the complete Hebrew alphabet. Some are missing one or more letters (*9, 10, 25, 34, 45*).
  - ▶ The most famous acrostic is *Psalm 119*.
    - ▷ It has 22 stanzas.
    - ▷ Each stanza has eight verses, for a total of 176 verses.
    - ▷ *Psalm 119* gives thanks for the many ways God guides His people through His Word. It uses eight different words to describe how God reveals Himself to man:
      - ✦ Law is used 25 times in *Psalm 119*. It refers to the first five books of the Old Testament.
      - ✦ Testimony is used 22 times. It refers to God's standard of conduct according to the Ten Commandments.
      - ✦ Way is used 11 times. It refers to the kind of life required by God's law.
      - ✦ Precepts is used 21 times. It means "requirements" or "commandments."
      - ✦ Statutes is also used 21 times. It refers to boundaries or laws that have been put into place.
      - ✦ Commandments is used 22 times. It refers to clear and authoritative orders.
      - ✦ Judgments is used 23 times. It means "binding laws" or "a judge's decision."
      - ✦ Word is used 39 times. It is a general term for God's revealing of Himself to people.[14]
        - → By making the Scriptures easier to memorize, the acrostic psalms helped people fulfill *Psalm 139:11*.

- Hallelujah Psalms: *113-118*.
  ▶ These psalms are still used at Passover celebrations as part of the retelling of God's deliverance of Israel from Egypt.
  ▶ *Psalms 113-114* are read at the beginning of the Passover ceremony, and *Psalms 115-118* are read at the end of the Passover meal.
- Messianic Psalms: *2, 8, 16, 22-24, 31, 34, 40, 41, 45, 55, 68, 69, 72, 89, 102, 109, 110, 118, 129*.
  ▶ The messianic psalms contain prophecies and references regarding Jesus Christ. The chart below shows a number of such passages from these psalms and how Christ fulfilled them in the New Testament:[15]

Messianic Prophecies in Psalms and Their Fulfillment

Prophecy	Reference in Psalms	New Testament Fulfillment
Christ's obedience	*40:6-10*	*Heb. 10:5-7*
Christ's zeal	*69:9*	*Joh. 2:17*
Christ's rejection	*118:22*	*Mat. 21:42*
Christ's betrayal	*41:9; 55:12-14*	*Mat. 26:14-16, 21-25*
Christ's sufferings	*22:1, 6-8; 69:21; 31:5; 34:20; 129:3*	*Mat. 27:34, 48; Luk. 23:46; Joh. 19:33-36*
Christ's false witnesses	*109:2-3*	*Mat. 26:59-61; 27:39-44*
Christ's prayers for enemies	*109:4*	*Luk. 23:34*
Christ's resurrection	*16:10; 22:22*	*Act. 13:35; Joh. 20:17*
Christ's ascension	*68:18*	*Eph. 4:8*
Christ's triumphal entry	*24:7-8*	*Joh. 12:12-16; Act. 1*
Christ's high priestly work	*110:4*	*Heb. 5-7*
Christ's marriage	*45:2, 6, 8, 13, 15*	*Rev. 19*
Christ's destruction of the heathen	*110:1, 6*	*Rev. 6-19*
Christ's millennial reign	*89:27; 102:16-21; 8:6; 72:17*	*Heb. 2; Mat. 23:39; Rev. 11:15*

▶ *Psalm 22* is a messianic psalm that predicts events of Christ's crucifixion in amazing detail.
  ▷ *22:1* was quoted by Christ on the cross: *"My God, My God, why have You forsaken Me?"* (Mat. 27:46)
  ▷ *22:8* was quoted by the Israelite rulers at the cross *"He trusted in the LORD, let Him rescue Him; Let Him deliver Him, since He delights in Him!"* (Mat: 27:43)
  ▷ *22:16* was fulfilled by Roman soldiers at the cross: *"They pierced My hands and My feet."* (Mat. 27:35)
  ▷ *22:18* was also fulfilled by Roman soldiers at the cross: *"They divide My garments among them, and for My clothing they cast lots."* (Mar. 15:24)
  ▷ *22:22* is quoted in *Heb. 2:12*. It tells about the glory that followed Jesus' suffering on the cross. *"I will declare Your name to My brethren; in the midst of the assembly I will praise You."*
  ▷ The Psalms are sometimes called "the heart of the Old Testament"

NOTES for the riches of worship, wisdom and prophecy they contain. David wrote almost half the psalms we have in the Bible, and was clearly used by God to bless us through the book of Psalms.

Questions:

Which type of psalm (acrostic, devotional, messianic, etc.) would help you most in reaching the people to whom you teach or preach? Why?

Which story from David's life reminds you most of people's lives where you live?

How would you use the story to share the Gospel with someone? Please use Scripture to support your answer.

C. **Solomon** (*1 Kin. 1-11; 2 Chr. 1-9.* Solomon's reign lasted from 970-930 BC).
- As David died, he told Solomon to do the following things (*1 Kin. 2*):
  ▶ Act like a man of God.
  ▶ Live by God's Word.
  ▶ Trust God's promises.
  ▶ Carry out God's judgment.
- Solomon's rule began with competition for the throne of Israel from his half-brother Adonijah (*1 Kin. 1-2*).
  ▶ David said that Solomon was to replace him as king of Israel.
  ▶ Solomon's supporters crowned him king in a public ceremony. This made Adonijah and his supporters afraid.
  ▶ After David died, Adonijah was exiled, and then executed.
- Solomon is visited by the Lord in a dream. God tells him he can have anything he desires. Solomon asked God for wisdom above all else. God answered Solomon's prayer with favor (*1 Kin. 3:4-28*).
- Solomon's early reign was peaceful and prosperous (*1 Kin. 4*).
  ▶ In seven years, Solomon led Israel in completing the temple. The temple was twice the size of the tabernacle (*1 Kin. 5-8; 2 Chr. 2-7*).
    ▷ Solomon prayed that the temple would influence individuals, Israel, and the nations to honor God.
- Solomon built up great riches during his rule (*1 Kin. 4:26; 9:17, 26-28; 10:22, 26; 11:3*).

- Besides 700 wives and 300 concubines, Solomon had
  - Massive amounts of gold.
  - 40,000 horses.
  - 1,400 chariots.
  - Many ships.
  - A huge ivory throne covered with gold.
  - 12,000 horsemen at his command.
- Solomon's wisdom was tested and proven in a wide range of subjects. He was known for his wisdom in natural science, engineering, business, philosophy, architecture, and more (*1 Kin. 4:29-34; 10:1-13; Ecc. 2:3-5*).
  - The Queen of Sheba came to test the wealth and wisdom of Solomon in person. She said that what she saw was greater than what she had heard about Solomon (*1 Kin. 1:7*).
- Solomon is known for writing all or part of several books in the Bible.
  - Solomon had a significant part in writing Proverbs.
    - A proverb is a short saying that gives wisdom and insight to those who hear it.
    - The book of Proverbs has several authors.
      - Solomon wrote *Proverbs 1-24*.
        - *1 Kin. 4:32* says Solomon wrote 3,000 proverbs and over 1,000 songs. That means *Proverbs 1-24* has only a small portion of Solomon's proverbs.
      - A group called "the men of Hezekiah" wrote *Proverbs 25-29*.
      - A wise man named Agur wrote *Proverbs 30*.
      - A leader named Lemuel wrote *Proverbs 31*.
    - Solomon and the other authors of Proverbs wrote about ten main topics. These include:[16]
    - A good name:
      - "*The memory of the righteous is blessed, but the name of the wicked will rot.*" (*10:7*)
      - "*A good name is to be chosen rather than great riches, loving favor rather than silver and gold.*" (*22:1*)
    - Youth and discipline:
      - "*He who spares his rod hates his son, but he who loves him disciplines him promptly.*" (*13:24*)
      - "*Train up a child in the way he should go, and when he is old he will not depart from it.*" (*22:6*)
    - Business matters:
      - "*Dishonest scales are an abomination to the LORD, but a just weight is His delight.*" (*11:1*)
      - "*As vinegar to the teeth and smoke to the eyes, so is the lazy man to those who send him.*" (*10:26*)
    - Marriage:
      - "*Let your fountain be blessed, and rejoice with the wife of your youth.*" (*5:18*).
      - "*Who can find a virtuous wife? For her worth is far above rubies.*" (*31:10*).
    - Immorality:
      - "*For the lips of an immoral woman drip honey, and her mouth is smoother than oil; But in the end she is bitter as worm-*

NOTES

wood, Sharp as a two-edged sword. Her feet go down to death, Her steps lay hold of hell." (5:3-5)
- Wisdom:
  - "Happy is the man who finds wisdom, and the man who gains understanding." (3:13)
  - "For whoever finds [wisdom] finds life, and obtains favor from the LORD." (8:35)
- Self-control:
  - "He who is slow to anger is better than the mighty, and he who rules his spirit than he who takes a city." (16:32)
  - "Whoever has no rule over his own spirit is like a city broken down, without walls." (25:28)
- Strong drink:
  - "Wine is a mocker, strong drink is a brawler, and whoever is led astray by it is not wise." (20:1)
- Friendship:
  - "A friend loves at all times, and a brother is born for adversity." (17:17)
  - "A man who has friends must himself be friendly, but there is a friend who sticks closer than a brother." (18:24)
  - "Faithful are the wounds of a friend, but the kisses of an enemy are deceitful." (27:6)
- Words and the tongue:
  - "A soft answer turns away wrath, but a harsh word stirs up anger." (15:1)
  - "A man has joy by the answer of his mouth, and a word spoken in due season, how good it is." (15:23)
  - "The heart of the righteous studies how to answer, but the mouth of the wicked pours forth evil." (15:28)

▶ In Ecclesiastes, Solomon says that even with God, life is a mystery. However, life without God is terrible. The best way through life is to fear God and keep His commandments.
- Ecclesiastes means "to address an assembly."
- Solomon's purpose in writing Ecclesiastes was to point people away from confidence in themselves and their own abilities, and point them toward faith in God as the only foundation for meaning in life.[17]
- Ecclesiastes also records man's faulty arguments about the meaning of life. Some of these places include:
  - "What is crooked cannot be made straight, and what is lacking cannot be numbered." (1:15)
  - "Nothing is better for a man than that he should eat and drink, and that his soul should enjoy good in his labor. This also, I saw, was from the hand of God." (2:24)
  - "For what happens to the sons of men also happens to animals; one thing befalls them: as one dies, so dies the other. Surely, they all have one breath; man has no advantage over animals, for all is vanity." (3:19).[18]
- In many ways, Ecclesiastes records Solomon's search for meaning in life. It begins by stating man's problems:

- Life seems futile: Though the translation uses the word vanity, a better translation is that life is but a vapor. Life is short, a vapor, it is here today and gone tomorrow. (*1:2*)
- Generations come and go and seem to make no difference: *"One generation passes away, and another generation comes but the earth abides forever."* (*1:4*)
- The sun rises and sets. The wind travels back and forth. The waters flow into the sea, back into the rivers, and back into the sea. It all makes no difference (*1:5-7*).
- Solomon had tried many things to bring meaning and enjoyment to his life:
  - Human wisdom (*1:16-17*).
  - Pleasure (*2:1-3*).
  - Alcohol (*2:3*).
  - Building projects, gardens, and parks (*2:4-6*).
  - Personal indulgences and wealth (*2:7-8*).
  - The arts (*2:8; 1 Kin. 4:32-33*).
- Yet Solomon found that none of those things meant anything without God. Life apart from God:
  - Was without meaning (*2:11*).
  - Repeated itself (*3:1-8*).
  - Was full of sorrow (*4:1*).
  - Was frustrating (*2:17*).
  - Was uncertain (*9:11-12*).
  - Was without purpose (*4:2-3*).
  - Was unjust (*7:15; 8:14*).
  - Was like the life of animals (*3:19*).
- Solomon's conclusion was that life is best if man finds God early in life (*11:9-10; 12:1-2*), and fears God throughout his life (*12:3-14*).
  ▷ Most scholars believe that Solomon wrote Ecclesiastes toward the end of his life, when he had the experience to know that God had to be the foundation of any life worth living.
► Solomon also wrote <u>Song of Solomon</u>, which celebrates love between a bride and bridegroom. It can also be a picture of the Bridegroom Jesus Christ and his Bride, the Church.
  ▷ Although God is not mentioned by name in Song of Solomon, the book reflects His design for the enjoyment of marriage between a man and a woman.
- Solomon's possessions and wives finally turned him away from God. He disobeyed the commands in the Law of Moses about kings not accumulating too much personal wealth (*1 Kin. 11; Deu. 17:14-17*).
  ► There were two consequences of Solomon's sin in this area.
    ▷ Troublemakers and minor revolts in Israel.
    ▷ After Solomon's death, God would take a large portion of Israel from Solomon's son and give it to someone else.
- Solomon died in 930 BC, following a 40-year reign as king of Israel.

Questions:

Review the lives of Saul, David and Solomon. Write down what you think were each king's main strength and main weakness. Support your answers with at least one Bible verse each.

Saul

Strength:

Weakness:

David

Strength:

Weakness:

Solomon

Strength:

Weakness:

In *1 Samuel 16:7*, God reminds Samuel that He looks at what is in men's hearts rather than how they look on the outside. What do you think God wants to find in people's hearts today? How can people develop hearts that please God? Use Scripture to support your answer.

Solomon had so many blessings yet ended up far from God. How did Solomon become distracted from God and His ways? How is Solomon's story like that of the world today? Use Scripture to support your answers.

Since life here on earth is a vapor, how can you train your people in your church plant to live life in Jesus with proper priorities?

Chapter Seven
The Chaotic Kingdom Stage

1. Chaotic Kingdom Stage Overview

A. The Chaotic Kingdom Stage covers the time from 931-605 BC, and 1 Kings 12-22, 2 Kings 1-17, 2 Chronicles 10-36, Obadiah, Joel, Jonah, Amos, Hosea, Micah, Isaiah, Nahum, Zephaniah, Habakkuk, Jeremiah, and Lamentations.
- This stage begins with a civil war shortly after Solomon's death that splits Israel into two opposing kingdoms. It ends with the capture of the southern kingdom (Judah) by the Babylonians.

B. The key people in the Chaotic Kingdom Stage are:
- The northern kings: Jeroboam, Omri, Ahab, Jehu, Jeroboam II, and Hoshea.
- The southern kings: Rehoboam, Asa, Jehoshaphat, Uzziah, Ahaz, Hezekiah, Manasseh, Josiah, Jehoiakim, and Zedekiah.
- The prophets: Elijah, Elisha, Obadiah, Joel, Jonah, Amos, Hosea, Isaiah, Micah, Nahum, Zephaniah, Jeremiah, and Habakkuk.

C. The key events in the Chaotic Kingdom Stage are:
- Israel's civil war.
- The Assyrian capture of the northern kingdom.
- Jerusalem's salvation from the Assyrians.
- The great preaching ministries of the prophets.
- The giving of the new covenant.
- The capture of the southern kingdom by the Babylonians.

D. The locations of the key events in this stage are:
- Israel's civil war: Palestine.
- The Assyrian capture of the northern kingdom: Samaria.
- Jerusalem's salvation from the Assyrians: Jerusalem.
- The great preaching ministries of the prophets: the northern and southern kingdoms, Babylon (Lamentations) and Nineveh (Jonah).

E. There are other important events in this stage.
- God's Word is discovered in the temple during the time of King Josiah, and Judah has a revival (*2 Kin. 22*).
- The Samaritan people are first identified (*2 Kin. 17*).
- Elijah defeats the prophets of Baal on Mt. Carmel (*1 Kin. 18:20-40*).
- Assyria's capital city Nineveh repents when it hears God's warning from Jonah (*Jon. 3*).

2. The Bible Account of the Chaotic Kingdom Stage

A. **Introduction**
- Solomon taxed all of Israel to help build the temple in the southern city of Jerusalem. This made the tribes of the northern part of Israel angry. The

NOTES

temple was not in their part of the kingdom. So they questioned why they should be taxed for it. After Solomon's death, the people of Israel asked his son Rehoboam for tax relief. Rehoboam said no. A civil war then divided Israel into two nations, the northern and southern kingdoms.

- The northern kingdom had 19 kings over a period of 210 years from 931-721 BC.
  ▶ The northern kings were:
    ▷ Jeroboam
    ▷ Nadab
    ▷ Baasha
    ▷ Elah
    ▷ Zimri
    ▷ Omri
    ▷ Ahab
    ▷ Ahaziah
    ▷ Jehoram
    ▷ Jehu
    ▷ Jehoahaz
    ▷ Jehoash
    ▷ Jeroboam II
    ▷ Zechariah
    ▷ Shallum
    ▷ Menahem
    ▷ Pekahiah
    ▷ Pekah
    ▷ Hoshea
  ▶ The northern kingdom is also called "Israel" or "Ephraim."
  ▶ The northern kingdom represented all the tribes of Israel except Judah and Benjamin.
  ▶ Its capital was Samaria.
  ▶ It was captured by the Assyrians in 721 BC.
  ▶ There was no return from its captivity.
- The southern kingdom had 20 kings over a period of 325 years from 931-606 BC.
  ▶ The southern kings were:
    ▷ Rehoboam
    ▷ Abijam
    ▷ Asa
    ▷ Jehoshaphat
    ▷ Jehoram
    ▷ Ahaziah
    ▷ Athaliah
    ▷ Joash
    ▷ Amaziah
    ▷ Uzziah
    ▷ Jotham
    ▷ Ahaz
    ▷ Hezekiah
    ▷ Manasseh
    ▷ Amon
    ▷ Josiah
    ▷ Jehoahaz
    ▷ Jehoiakim
    ▷ Jehoiachin
    ▷ Zedekiah
  ▶ The southern kingdom was also called "Judah."
  ▶ It consisted of two tribes, Judah and Benjamin.
  ▶ Its capital was Jerusalem.
  ▶ The southern kingdom was captured by the Babylonians in 606 BC.
  ▶ There were three separate returns of southern kingdom descendants from Babylon.

B. **The Northern Rulers of the Chaotic Kingdom**
- **Jeroboam** (*1 Kin. 11:26-14:20; 2 Chr. 9:29-13:22.* Twenty-two years in power from 931-909 BC). Jeroboam served in Solomon's court. He fled Israel for Egypt after the prophet Ahijah told him ten tribes of Israel would be torn from Solomon's hand and given to him.
  ▶ After Solomon died, Jeroboam led the revolt of the ten tribes at Shechem against Solomon's son Rehoboam.

▷ To keep his power after the revolt, Jeroboam turned his followers away from the worship of God to a false religion he created.
- Jeroboam changed the two cherubim on the Ark of the Covenant to two golden calves (*1 Kin. 12:28*; see *Exo. 32:4*).
- Jeroboam made priests of men who were not from the tribe of Levi. This caused most of the priests and Levites to move to Judah (*1 Kin. 12:31*), leaving people with little or no knowledge of the proper worship of God.
- Jeroboam changed the worship center from Jerusalem to Bethel and Dan (*1 Kin. 11:36*).
- Jeroboam directly disobeyed God, Who had commanded to bring all Israel to worship in Jerusalem three times a year.
- Jeroboam's false religion caused Israel to sin.

▷ God punished Jeroboam's wickedness.
- Jeroboam's altar to idols was destroyed.
- Jeroboam's arm was paralyzed.
- Jeroboam's son was given a sickness as a result of Jeroboam's sin.
- Abijam, the second king of the southern kingdom, defeated Jeroboam in battle.

▷ God caused Jeroboam to suffer a fatal plague.

Question:

Jeroboam's example shows us the trouble that comes when man tries to maintain his own power rather than honor God's power. In what ways do people try to hold on to their own power rather than honor God's power today? Discuss.

- **Nadab** (*1 Kin. 15:25-28*. Two years in power from 910-908 BC). Nadab was Jeroboam's son. A rebel named Baasha assassinated him and became king in his place.
- **Baasha** (*1 Kin. 15:27-16:7; 2 Chr. 16:1-6*. Twenty-four years in power from 909-885 BC). When Baasha killed Nadab he fulfilled Ahijah the prophet's prediction about Jeroboam's family (*1 Kin. 14:4, 15:29*).
  ▶ Baasha fought with Asa, the third king of the south.
    ▷ Baasha built a wall to cut off trade to Jerusalem.
  ▶ It was predicted that Baasha's family would suffer the same judgment as Jeroboam's.
- **Elah** (*1 Kin. 16:6-14*. Two years in power from 885-883 BC). Elah, the son of Baasha, was assassinated by a soldier rebel. This fulfilled the prophecy about Nadab's family.
- **Zimri** (*1 Kin. 16:9-20*. Seven days in power in 885 BC). Zimri was the assassin that fulfilled the prophecy about Nadab's family. He was trapped by rebel soldiers in his own palace. He burned down the palace, killing himself in the process.

NOTES
- **Omri** (*1 Kin. 16:15-28*. Twelve years in power from 885-873 BC). Omri made Samaria the capital of the northern kingdom.
  - He was the most powerful king up to his time, but he did not follow God's ways.
  - He arranged the marriage of his son Ahab to Jezebel.
- **Ahab** (*1 Kin. 16:28-22:40, 2 Chr. 18:1-34*. Twenty-two years in power from 874-852 BC). Ahab married Jezebel and brought Baal worship into Israel.
  - His practice of Baal worship caused famine in the northern kingdom.
  - The prophet Elijah often told Ahab that God's judgment on Israel was due to its idolatry.
    - Ahab was the king of Israel when the prophet Elijah challenged the priests of Baal to a contest on Mt. Carmel to determine which god was truly God (*1 Kin. 18*). Elijah defeated and destroyed the priests of Baal in this contest.
    - Ahab also loved wealth more than justice. He wanted the vineyard of a man named Naboth. Naboth did not want to sell his vineyard. Yet Jezebel created a series of lies about Naboth that led to the death of Naboth and his sons. This allowed Ahab to take the vineyard (*1 Kin. 21:4-14*).
      - For their plans and lies against Naboth, God commanded Elijah to pronounce judgment on Ahab and his family (*1 Kin. 21:19-24*). Each of these prophecies were fulfilled:
        - The dogs would lick Ahab's blood (*1 Kin. 22:38*).
        - Ahab's sons would be killed (*2 Kin. 1:17, 9:24*).
        - Jezebel would be eaten by the wild dogs of Jezreel (*2 Kin. 9:30-36*).
  - Ahab tricked the fourth king of Judah (Jehoshaphat), into military and personal compromises.
  - He was successful in early battles against Syria, but he was rebellious against God. Yet Ahab did have some sort of conversion experience (1 Kin. 21:29).
    - Against God's command, Ahab spared Syria's king Ben-Hadad. God told Ahab his disobedience would cost him his life (*1 Kin. 20:32-43*).
    - Three years later, Ahab was killed in a battle with Syria (*1 Kin. 22:29-37*).
    - Ahab was buried in Samaria. As Elijah had predicted, dogs licked his blood from his chariot as it was being cleaned (*1 Kin. 22:38-39*).

Question:

Ahab tried many things to avoid the consequences of his actions against God. What are some ways people use today to try to avoid the consequences of their sins? How can we misuse power as a church planter? What is the difference between Biblical authority, and power as you know it in your own context? Discuss.

- **Ahaziah** (*1 Kin. 22:40-2 Kin. 1:18; 2 Chr. 20:35-37*. Two years in power from 853-851 BC). Ahaziah was the oldest son of Ahab and Jezebel. He continued in the evil ways of his father Ahab.
  - ▶ He started a ship-building business with Jehoshaphat at Ezion-Geber.
  - ▶ Ahaziah was badly injured from a fall in his palace at Samaria.
    - ▷ Instead of asking the true God for healing, Ahaziah asked the pagan god Baal-Zebub for healing.
    - ▷ The prophet Elijah rebuked Ahaziah for his idol worship.
    - ▷ Ahaziah died soon after his fall.
- **Jehoram** (*2 Kin. 3:1-9:25; 2 Chr. 22:5-7*. Twelve years in power from 852-840 BC). Jehoram was the youngest son of Ahab and Jezebel. He talked Jehoshaphat into taking sides with him against Syria.
  - ▶ Elisha performed a miracle which won the battle for Jehoshaphat's sake.
  - ▶ Elisha also helped Jehoram by warning him about Syrian ambushes against him.
  - ▶ He saw God working for Israel when four lepers saved Samaria from starvation.
  - ▶ Jehu murdered Jehoram in the Valley of Jezreel.
- **Jehu** (*2 Kin. 9:1-10:36; 2 Chr. 22:7-12*. Twenty-eight years in power from 841-813 BC). Jehu was anointed by a messenger from the prophet Elisha. He often brought God's judgment to bear on those who worshiped other gods. Jehu killed the following people:
  - ▶ King Ahaziah of the southern kingdom, the grandson of Jehoshaphat.
  - ▶ Jehoram, the northern king.
  - ▶ Jezebel.
  - ▶ Ahab's seventy sons, relatives, and friends.
  - ▶ Forty-two royal princes of Judah.
  - ▶ Baal-worshipers.
    - ▷ Although God had commanded Jehu to execute Ahab's family, He did not tell Jehu to kill any of the others.
    - ▷ Because Jehu obeyed God about the destruction of Ahab's family, God promised Jehu that his family would rule for four generations (*2 Kin. 10:30*).
  - ▶ Jehu also killed the priests of Baal as they met in Jezreel. He burned their altar, destroyed their temple, and turned the temple into a public toilet.
  - ▶ Yet Jehu himself continued to worship the golden calves set up by Jeroboam.

Question:

Jehu did many things that showed his obedience to God. But there are other actions he took that show Jehu was not a close follower of God. How will you as a leader of the Lord's church keep from being half-hearted? Support your answers with Scripture.

NOTES

- **Jehoahaz** (*2 Kin. 13:1-9*. Seventeen years in power from 814-797 BC). Jehoahaz was the son of Jehu. Syria almost completely destroyed Israel's army during Jehoahaz' reign. Jehoahaz felt remorse for his sins for a brief time. Yet it seems that he never truly repented.
- **Jehoash** (*2 Kin. 13:10-14:16; 2 Chr. 25:17-24*. Sixteen years in power from 798-782 BC). Jehoash, the son of Jehoahaz, visited the prophet Elisha on his deathbed. Jehoash took many hostages and great wealth out of Jerusalem.
- **Jeroboam II** (*2 Kin. 14:23-29*. Forty-one years in power from 793-752 BC). Jeroboam II was one of the most powerful kings of the north. He recovered much of the land Israel had lost to the Syrians. Yet he did evil in God's sight by not destroying the idols in the land.
  - ▶ The prophet Jonah lived during the reign of Jeroboam II. He predicted that Jeroboam II would restore most of Israel's land (*2 Kin. 14:25*).
- **Zechariah** (*2 Kin. 14:29-15:12*. Six months in power in 753 BC). Zechariah was the great-great-grandson of Jehu. The rebel Shallum murdered Zechariah, fulfilling God's prophecy against Jehu and his family line (see *2 Kin. 10:30, 14:29, 15:8-12*).
- **Shallum** (*2 Kin. 15:10-15*. One month in power in 752 BC). A few weeks after he became king, Shallum was murdered by a soldier named Menahem.
- **Menahem** (*2 Kin. 15:14-22*. Ten years in power from 752-742 BC). Menahem was an evil and violent king.
- **Pekahiah** (*2 Kin. 15:22-26*. Two years in power from 742-740 BC). Pekehiah, the son of Menahem, was killed by his army commander Pekah.
- **Pekah** (*2 Kin. 15:27-31, 2 Chr. 28:5-8*. Twenty years in power from 740-732 BC). Pekah probably shared the rule of the northern kingdom with both Menahem and Pekahiah for twelve years.
  - ▶ Pekah joined sides with Syria.
  - ▶ Assyria captured some of Israel's northern and eastern cities during Pekah's reign.
  - ▶ Pekah was assassinated by Hoshea.
- **Hoshea** (*2 Kin. 15:30-17:6*. Nine years in power from 732-721 BC). Hoshea was the last king of the northern kingdom.
  - ▶ He joined with Egypt to rebel against Assyria. For this, Assyria imprisoned Hoshea.
  - ▶ The people of Israel were then exiled to Assyria.
- The King of Assyria brought people from other lands into northern Israel to start Assyrian colonies (*2 Kin. 17:24*).
  - ▶ God sent a plague of man-eating lions into the colonies. The people there asked the Assyrian ruler for a priest to stop the lions. This priest taught them how to fear the Lord.
  - ▶ A prophet arrived from Bethel. The plague soon stopped. But the people combined worship of Jehovah with idol worship (*2 Kin. 17:27-34*).
  - ▶ These people became the Samaritans (see *John 4*).

Questions:

What have you experienced with people who combine the worship of other gods with the worship of the true God? Show from the Scriptures whether or not God tolerates this behavior.

What should our response be when we see the combined worship of the true God and other gods today? Discuss.

C. **The Southern Kings of the Chaotic Kingdom**
  - **Rehoboam** (*1 Kin. 11:42-14:31; 2 Chr. 9:31-12:16*. Seventeen years in power from 931-914 BC). Rehoboam was the son of Solomon. His stubborn attitude caused the civil war of Israel that resulted in its split into two kingdoms.
    ▶ He had 18 wives and 60 concubines. Foreign wives and lovers probably made Rehoboam more accepting of foreign customs and gods. His favorite wife, Maachah, was an idol worshiper who influenced Rehoboam to build places for idol worship throughout Judah. Sexual sin was also common during Rehoboam's time as king.
    ▶ Because of Rehoboam's wickedness Shishak, the Pharaoh of Egypt, invaded Jerusalem.
      ▷ Jerusalem was spared because of a nation-wide revival in Judah.
      ▷ Yet, Shisak takes treasure from the temple in Jerusalem. Judah was unable to replace the treasure Shisak took. This showed that Judah was in decay spiritually and financially.
  - **Abijam** (*1 Kin. 14:31-15:8; 2 Chr. 13:1-22*. Three years in power from 914-911 BC). With God's help Abijam defeated the northern king Jeroboam in battle. But Abijam forgot God, and became a wicked king.
  - **Asa** (*1 Kin. 15:8-14; 2 Chr. 14:1-16:14*. Forty-one years in power from 911-870 BC). Asa followed God's ways for most of his reign.
    ▶ He led Judah in a revival (*2 Chr. 14:2-5*).
    ▶ Asa built up and fenced in Judah's cities (*2 Chr. 14:6-7*).
    ▶ God answered his prayer for rescue from a large attack on Jerusalem by Ethiopia (*2 Chr. 14:9-12*).
    ▶ Asa took away his own grandmother's royal treatment because she worshiped idols (*1 Kin. 15:13*).
    ▶ Yet Asa later fell away from God.
      ▷ He put a prophet who warned him about his sin into prison (*2 Chr. 16:8-10*).
      ▷ Asa died from a foot disease. He refused to ask God to heal him.
  - **Jehoshaphat** (*1 Kin. 22:41-50; 2 Chr. 17:1-20:37*. Twenty-five years in power from 873-848 BC). Jehoshaphat sent out teachers of God's Word into Judah to instruct the nation about God and His ways.

NOTES

- He had both a religious director and a civil director in his government. He saw the need to support both religion and the state.
- Yet he joined with three evil northern kings (Ahab and his sons Ahaziah and Jehoram) in family, military and trading alliances.
- When Moab wanted to invade Jerusalem, Jehoshaphat led Judah in a time of national prayer and fasting. He prayed:

    O LORD God of our fathers, are You not God in heaven, and do You not rule over all the kingdoms of the nations, and in Your hand is there not power and might, so that no one is able to withstand You?... and now, here are the people of Ammon, Moab, and Mount Seir whom You would not let Israel invade when they came out of the land of Egypt, but they turned from them and did not destroy them-here they are, rewarding us by coming to throw us out of Your possession which You have given us to inherit. O our God, will You not judge them? For we have no power against this great multitude that is coming against us; nor do we know what to do, but our eyes are upon You (2 Chr. 20:6, 10-12).

    - God heard Jehoshaphat's prayer. The next morning, Judah goes to battle with a choir leading the way singing, *"His mercy endures forever."* (*2 Chr. 20:21*) God confused the enemies of Israel so much that they began fighting among themselves. Israel won the battle with worship rather than weapons of war that day.

- **Jehoram** (*2 Kin. 8:16-24; 2 Chr. 21:1-20*. Eight years in power from 853-845 BC). Jehoram married Athaliah, the daughter of Ahab and Jezebel. He murdered his six brothers as he came to power.
    - Elijah sent a letter to warn Jehoram about God's coming judgment on him.
    - Jehoram was defeated by the Philistines and Arabians.
    - God struck him with a fatal intestinal disease.
- **Ahaziah** (*2 Kin. 8:24-9:29; 2 Chr. 22:1-9*. One year in power during 841 BC). Ahaziah was the son of Jehoram and Athaliah. He was killed by Jehu, the tenth northern king.
- **Athaliah** (*2 Kin. 11:1-20; 2 Chr. 22:1-23:21*. Six years in power from 841-835 BC). Athaliah took over the rule of Judah when her son Ahaziah died.
- **Joash** (*2 Kin. 11:1-12:21; 2 Chr. 22:10-24:27*. Forty years in power from 835-795 BC). Joash lived for God in his early years, but later turned away from God.
    - While the high priest Jehoiada was alive, Joash destroyed many temples of Baal in Judah. He also ordered Jehoiada to repair the temple of God.
    - After Jehoiada died, the leaders of Judah convinced Joash to ignore God and worship idols.
    - Judah's high priest Zechariah spoke out about Joash's sin of idolatry and called for Judah to repent. Joash ordered Zechariah's death.
        - Jesus refers to this event in *Matthew 23:35*.
- **Amaziah (*2 Kin. 14:1-20; 2 Chr. 25:1-28*.** Twenty-nine years in power from 796-767 BC). Amaziah executed the killers of his father Joash, He hired mercenary soldiers from Israel to help him fight Edom.

- **Uzziah** (*2 Kin. 15:1-7; 2 Chr. 26:1-23*. Fifty-two years in power from 792-740 BC). Uzziah was a very successful builder and warrior.
  - ▶ Uzziah became a proud man, which led to his personal downfall (*2 Chr.26:16*). Uzziah was also known as "Azariah."

Question:

Uzziah made wise decisions as a king, but not as a follower of God. Jehoshaphat made wise decisions as a follower of God, but not always as a king. Would you rather have a leader be like Uzziah or Jehoshaphat? Discuss.

- **Jotham** (*2 Kin. 15:32-38; 2 Chr. 27:1-9*. Sixteen years in power from 750-736 BC). Jotham was a good king. He defeated the enemies of Judah and received huge payments from them each year.
- **Ahaz** (*2 Kin. 16:1-20; 2 Chr. 28:1-27*. Sixteen years in power from 735-719 BC). Ahaz was very evil.
  - ▶ Even after the prophet Isaiah assured him that God would destroy his enemies, Ahaz became a Baal worshiper.
    - ▷ He sacrificed his own children to false gods.
    - ▷ He used gold and silver from the temple treasury to bribe the Assyrian king Tiglath-Pileser.
- **Hezekiah** (*2 Kin. 18:1-20:21; 2 Chr. 29:1-32:33*. Twenty nine years in power from 716-687 BC). Hezekiah was the richest and one of the best kings of Judah.
  - ▶ Hezekiah helped restore things that led people to worship the living and true God.
    - ▷ He destroyed shrines and idols that people were worshiping in place of God.
    - ▷ He repaired the temple.
    - ▷ He hosted a great Passover celebration.
    - ▷ As revival spread, people tithed and gave generously. The temple treasury was more than filled.
  - ▶ Hezekiah also had military success.
    - ▷ He rebelled against Assyria and no longer gave them an annual payment.
    - ▷ Toward the end of his life, Hezekiah saw the death angel of the Lord defeat the Assyrian armies that surrounded Jerusalem.
  - ▶ God healed Hezekiah of a deadly disease. This gave Hezekiah another 15 years of life.
    - ▷ In response, Hezekiah added 15 psalms that are in the Bible today.
    - ▷ Hezekiah also asked and received a sign from God that his healing would take place: God moved the shadow on the royal sundial back ten points.

NOTES

NOTES

- ▷ Hezekiah wrote a journal during his sickness. Isaiah included a page from this journal in the book of Isaiah (*Isa. 38:9-20*).
- ▶ In a foolish moment, Hezekiah showed Judah's wealth to some Babylonian officials.
  - ▷ Isaiah did not approve of this. He told the king the Babylonians would take Judah captive someday to get the treasure Hezekiah had shown them.

Question:

Hezekiah showed his gratitude to God in worship and in giving. What are some specific ways you show your gratitude to God for the blessings He gives you today? Discuss.

- **Manasseh** (*2 Kin. 21:1-18; 2 Chr. 33:1-20*. Fifty-five years in power from 697-642 BC). Manasseh ruled longer than any other king of Judah or Israel.
  - ▶ The Bible says Manasseh was the most evil king of all.
    - ▷ He rebuilt the altars to Baal his father had destroyed.
    - ▷ He set up a place to worship the sun, moon and stars in the house of God.
    - ▷ He sacrificed his own children to idols and shed innocent blood.
    - ▷ He ignored God's warnings to change (*2 Chr. 33:10*).
  - ▶ Yet he came to faith in God while he was in an enemy prison.
    - ▷ He was allowed to return to Judah as its king.
- **Amon** (*2 Kin. 21:19-26, 2 Chr. 33:21-25*. Two years in power from 643-641 BC). Amon was wicked like his father Manasseh. Sadly, Amon did not repent like his father did. His own household servants killed him.
- **Josiah** (*2 Kin. 22:1-23:30, 2 Chr. 34:1-35:27*. Thirty-one years in power from 641-610 BC). Josiah was the godliest king since David. He is known as Judah's last godly king.
  - ▶ Josiah's reign began with the discovery of the book of Moses while the high priest Hilkiah was cleaning the temple.
    - ▷ Josiah used the instruction in the book to lead Judah in a great revival.
      - ✦ Throughout Judah and even in Israel, Josiah tore down the altars his father and grandfather had built for the worship of idols and foreign gods.
      - ✦ Josiah invited the priests of God living throughout Judah back to Jerusalem.
    - ▷ He also led Judah in a great Passover celebration.
    - ▷ He fulfilled a prophecy that predicted the destruction of an altar built by Jeroboam (see *1 Kin. 13:1-2* and *2 Kin. 23:15*).
  - ▶ Josiah was killed in battle against the Egyptians.

- **Jehoahaz** (*2 Kin. 23:31-33; 2 Chr. 36:1-4*. Three months in power during 609 BC). Jehoahaz was Josiah's son. After only 90 days in power, Jehoahaz was removed from Judah's throne by the Pharaoh who had killed his father.
- **Jehoiakim** (*2 Kin. 23:34-24:5, 2 Chr. 36:5-7*. Eleven years in power from 609-598 BC). Jehoiakim was the oldest brother of Jehoazaz. The Egyptian Pharaoh put Jehoiakim in power.
  - ▶ Jehoiakim tried to silence the prophets of God.
    - ▷ He murdered the prophet Uriah.
    - ▷ He constantly tried to silence Jeremiah.
  - ▶ Jehoiakim burned the scroll that had the inspired writings of Jeremiah. Jeremiah rewrote all the king had burned and added a prophecy against Jehoiakim.
  - ▶ When Babylon defeated Egypt, Judah became subject to Babylon's king Nebuchadnezzar.
    - ▷ Jehoiakim went through the first of three Babylonian captivities.
      - ◆ This first captivity, in 606 BC, was when Daniel and the other Hebrew youth were carried off to Babylon.
- **Jehoiachin** (*2 Kin. 24:6-16; 2 Chr. 36:8-10*. Three months in power during 598 BC). Jehoiachin was the grandson of Josiah and the son of Jehoiakim. God cursed this evil king, saying his sons would not sit on Judah's throne.
  - ▶ Both Ezekiel and Jeremiah predicted Jehoiachin would be carried off as a captive to Babylon (*Eze. 19:5-9; Jer. 22:24-26*).
    - ▷ This happened in the second "wave" of Babylonian captivity in 597 BC.
      - ◆ Ezekiel the prophet was also taken to Babylon at this time.
- **Zedekiah** (*2 Kin. 24:17-25:30, 2 Chr. 36:11-21*. Eleven years in power from 597-586 BC).
  - ▶ Zedekiah was in a constant struggle with the prophet Jeremiah.
    - ▷ Zedekiah hated Jeremiah's message of divine judgment (*Jer. 11:8-10*).
    - ▷ Zedekiah repeatedly put Jeremiah in prison (*Jer. 27:11-16; 37:21; 32:6-15*).
    - ▷ Zedekiah refused to hear Jeremiah's warning to submit to Babylon rather than rebel against it (*Jer. 38:14-26*).
  - ▶ Zedekiah finally joined Egypt to rebel against Babylon. As a result he was captured, blinded, and taken to Babylon by Nebuchadnezzar (*Jer. 52:4-11; 39:1-7*).
  - ▶ Jerusalem and the temple were burned to the ground at this time (*Jer. 52:12-23*).

3. The Prophets of the Chaotic Kingdom

A. **Elijah's** name means "The Lord Is My God." We know little about the prophet until he begins speaking to Ahab (*1 Kin. 17*). He spoke God's truth with force during the time of the northern kings Ahab, Ahaziah, and Jehoram (from about 874-853 BC).
- King Ahab was not a follower of God. Elijah had to bring messages of judgment to Ahab because Ahab would not turn away from his worship of Baal.

NOTES

- Elijah announced a three-and-a-half year drought on Israel to Ahab. Not a drop of rain would fall on Israel until Elijah said so (*1 Kin. 17:1*).
- Not much later, Elijah challenged Ahab to a contest on Mt. Carmel. The contest would show whether Baal or the Lord was the true God (*1 Kin. 17:17-19*).
- Elijah predicted the end of the drought on Israel (*1 Kin. 18:41-46*).
- Elijah also predicted the deaths of Ahab and his wife Jezebel (*1 Kin. 21:17-24*).

• God often led Elijah to the countryside when the prophet needed a place to rest or hide.
- After Elijah's announcement to Ahab about the drought, God told Elijah to hide near the Brook Cherith. Elijah would drink from the brook. God commanded the ravens there to feed him (*1 Kin. 17:2-7*).

• God then led Elijah to a poverty-stricken widow's house in the town of Zarephath. God provides flour and oil for the widow to feed her family and the prophet (*1 Kin. 17:8-16*).
- God also used Elijah to raise the widow's son from the dead (*1 Kin. 17:17-24*).
  ▷ Although the widow had shared what little she had with Elijah in faith, the death of her son was a hard test of her faith. As a widow without a son to help her, she would probably become a beggar.
  ▷ The widow affirmed that Elijah was a man of God. She said Elijah's faith in God was real (*17:18*).
  ▷ Elijah carried her son upstairs. He stretched himself over the boy's body three times. He prayed that God would raise the boy. God answered Elijah's prayer (*17:22*).
- A house servant of Ahab's named Obadiah (not the prophet) arranged a meeting between Elijah and Ahab. Here, Ahab says Elijah is the cause of all Israel's problems. Elijah says that Ahab's worship of idols and disobedience to God are the problems (*1 Kin. 18:1-19*).
  ▷ Elijah's contest on Mt. Carmel with the prophets of Baal is possibly the most important event in the prophet's ministry (*1 Kin. 18:20-40*).
    ◆ The living God would show his power by consuming the sacrifice dedicated to Him on Mt. Carmel with fire.
    ◆ Despite all the priests of Baal and their praying, dancing, agonizing, screaming, and even cutting themselves on Mt. Carmel, nothing happened to the sacrifice to Baal.
    ◆ Elijah poured 12 barrels of water on his sacrifice to the Lord. When he prayed, God sent fire and consumed Elijah's sacrifice.
    ◆ The people of Israel killed the prophets of Baal for leading them into the worship of a false god.
    ◆ After a sevenfold prayer meeting there was a great rain (*18:45*).
- Ahab's wife Jezebel wanted Elijah's life in exchange for the lives of all the priests of Baal. Elijah again escaped to the wilderness to hide and rest (*19:1-18*).
  ▷ An angel took care of Elijah.

▷ In a cave in the wilderness, God spoke to Elijah in a still small voice and ordered him to immediately do four things:
  ◆ Start preaching again.
  ◆ Anoint Hazael to be king of Syria.
  ◆ Anoint Jehu to be king of Israel.
  ◆ Begin training Elisha to succeed him.
▶ Elijah spent time with Elisha, the prophet who would someday take his place. He called Elisha away from his everyday life to prepare the younger man to serve as a prophet (*1 Kin. 19:19-21; 2 Kin. 2:1-10*).
▶ When God called Elijah to heaven, Elijah parted the River Jordan. He stood on the western bank. Elisha requested a double portion of Elijah's spirit. Elijah, without dying, was then taken into heaven by a chariot of fire (*2 Kin. 2:1-11*).

Questions:

Elijah was one of two men to never face death. Who was the other? (See *Gen. 5:24*).

Pick three words that you think describe Elijah. Support your answers with Scripture.

How has God provided for you when there were no resources in sight? Pray for your Elisha, your disciple that you can train to go beyond you in ministry fruitfulness.

What do you think Elijah would tell God's people today? Discuss.

B. **Elisha's** ministry as prophet lasted about half a century (from about 853-800 BC). Where Elijah was a man who was often alone, Elisha lived among the people.
  • Elisha's first miracle was to part the Jordan River by striking it with Elijah's cloak (*2 Kin. 2:14*). This confirmed that Elisha had received a double portion of Elijah's spirit.
  • Elisha then purified a bitter well at Jericho with a bowl of salt (*2:19-22*).

NOTES

NOTES

The water in the well had been a source of sickness for those who drank from it. It was pure from that day forward.

- When the allied armies of Judah and Israel met in Edom to fight Moab, they lacked water. Because Jehoshaphat of Judah followed God, Elisha ordered great ditches to be dug. The next day, God filled them all with water (*3:9-20*).
- Elisha was given a place to stay in Shunem by a respected couple in that city. Elisha prophesied the couple would have a son. The son was born, but some years later fell sick and died (*4:8-37*).
  - ▶ The mother found Elisha and asked for help.
  - ▶ First Elisha sent his servant Gehazi to the boy. Gehazi laid Elisha's staff on the boy's face but nothing happened.
  - ▶ Then Elisha went to the boy. He stretched his body over the child.
  - ▶ The boy sneezed seven times and opened his eyes.
- Elisha directed the Syrian commander Naaman to be cured of his leprosy by washing seven times in the Jordan River. This showed that the reach of God's mercy could extend beyond the people of Israel (*5:1-19*).
- When an ax head from a borrowed ax fell off into the Jordan, Elisha made the ax head float to get it back (*6:1-7*).
  - ▶ By making the ax head float, Elisha kept the man who borrowed the ax from becoming a slave.
- Elisha was part of three miracles with the Syrian army (*6:8-10*).
- Years later the Syrians surrounded Samaria and cut off their food supplies. The citizens were dying from hunger (*6:25-29*).
  - ▶ Jehoram blamed Elisha for the famine. He wanted to kill Elisha for not letting him kill the blinded Syrian soldiers from years before.
  - ▶ Elisha prophesied that within a day the famine would be over and food would be plentiful.
    - ▷ God caused the footsteps of four starving lepers outside Samaria's walls to sound like chariots and horses.
    - ▷ When they walked toward the Syrians to give themselves up, the Syrians thought they were the Hittites and Egyptians hired to fight them.
    - ▷ The Syrians ran away. The food supplies were immediately available (*2 Kin. 7*).
  - ▶ On his deathbed, Elisha predicted three victories by Israel over Syria (*13:14-19*). He told the king Jehoash to shoot an arrow from his bedroom window, which stood for Israel's victory over Syria.
    - ▷ Elisha then told Jehoash to strike the floor with some arrows. Jehoash struck the floor three times. Every strike meant another victory for Israel over Syria.
      - ◆ Jehoash went on to defeat the Syrians three times, just as Elisha said. (*13:22-25*).
  - ▶ The power of God was still on Elisha after he died. Years after Elisha was buried, another corpse was being buried. It touched Elisha's bones. The corpse revived and jumped to its feet (*13:20-21*).

NOTES

Questions:

The power of God was clear in Elisha's life and ministry through his prophecies and miracles. What are some ways the power of God is clear in your life?

What are some ways Elisha was like Elijah? What are some ways Elisha was different than Elijah? Support your answers with Scripture.

Name three important things from Elisha's ministry that we can apply to ministry today. Support your answers with Scripture.

C. **Obadiah** served 10 years as a prophet in Judah (850-840 BC), during the time of Jehoram. His message, which makes up the shortest and smallest Old Testament book, was aimed at Edom. Obadiah spoke of God's judgment that would destroy Edom because Edom had so often set itself against Judah in the past (*Obadiah 10-14*).[19] The lesson of Obadiah is to not set yourself against God's people and purposes.

D. **Joel** was in ministry as a prophet for seven years in Judah (841-834 BC), during the early reign of Joash. His message used a recent plague of locusts (*chapter 1*) to tell about the Day of the Lord and the coming judgment (*chapters 2, 3*).
  - Joel was also quoted by the apostle Peter on the Day of Pentecost (see *Act. 2:16-21* and *Joe. 2:28-32*).
  - One important message in Joel is about true repentance (*2:12-27*). Repentance is not an outward ritual. Rather it is the kind of grief over sin that breaks your heart, both as an individual and as a nation.

E. **Jonah** served 35 years as a prophet in the northern kingdom (785-750 BC), during the time of Jeroboam II. His message was for Nineveh, the capital of Assyria, to repent or to face destruction.
  - Jonah is famous as the prophet who responded to God's call to ministry by going in the other direction (*Jon. 1*). To correct Jonah's path, God sent a huge fish to swallow him and take him to God's destination at Nineveh.
  - Jonah repents of his own disobedience to God's call while in the belly of the fish (*Jon. 2*).
  - Jonah complained that it was probably worthless to try to give God's message to an evil place like Nineveh. But to Jonah's surprise, Nineveh repented (*Jon. 3*).
    ▶ Jesus later spoke with favor about Nineveh's repentance (*Mat. 12:41*).

NOTES

- Jonah was angry that God did not bring destruction upon the city. But God told the prophet that He would extend His mercy wherever He wanted (*Jon. 4*).
- Jonah's ministry helped Israel understand that God was interested in the people of Nineveh as well as Israel. The lesson of Jonah is that God wants everyone to turn to Him, whether or not His people believe them to be outsiders.

F. **Amos** served 7 years as a prophet mostly to the northern kingdom (760-753 BC) during the reigns of Uzziah in Judah and Jeroboam II of Israel. Amos' message told of the wickedness not only of Israel and Judah, but also of the nations surrounding them (*Amo. 1-2*).
- Under Jeroboam II, Israel had become wealthy as a nation. But those who had become personally wealthy wanted even more.
- The religious leaders of Amos' time did not speak out for God. They were part of a movement that favored the rich at the expense of the poor. Their religion had little to do with God's ways (*5:18-27; 7:10-13*).
- The rich people and rulers of Israel:
  ▶ Cheated small landowners (*2:6; 3:9-15*).
  ▶ Ran corrupt courts (*5:7, 12*).
  ▶ Required high-priced offerings for temple worship so corrupt priests would grow more wealthy (*5:21-23*).
  ▶ Demanded high prices for everyday supplies (*8:4-5*).
- Amos' message for Israel gave Israel the chance to repent. But repentance would mean Israel would have to practice justice and take care of the poor rather than cheat them (*5:4-6, 14-16*).
  ▶ God continues to call His people to treat their neighbors righteously and with love. This is one way others can see who truly belongs to God (*Mar. 12:30-34*).

G. **Hosea** was a prophet for up to 60 years in the northern kingdom (760-700 BC). This was during the time of the last six northern kings (from Jeroboam II to Hoshea), and after the Assyrian invasion of Samaria.
- Hosea not only predicted the Assyrian invasion of 721 BC, but he also lived to see it happen.
- God often said His relationship with Israel was like a marriage. Israel was being unfaithful in the marriage. Israel was committing itself to idols rather than to God (see *4:11-19*). So God told Hosea to marry an unfaithful woman (*Hos. 1*).
  ▶ Hosea's marriage to an unfaithful wife would be a living picture of the spiritual adultery Israel was committing against God.
  ▶ Because of his own feelings for his unfaithful wife, Hosea would better understand what God felt about Israel.
  ▶ Just like God loved Israel even though they were unfaithful, Hosea loved his wife Gomer even though she was unfaithful (*Hos. 2*).
  ▶ Just like Hosea wanted to restore his wife, God promised to restore Israel (*chapters 3, 11-14*).
    ▷ In Israel's case it meant being faithful to God and being just to their neighbors (*14:2-9*).

- They would give up their dependence on earthly power.
- They would completely turn away from idols and turn back to God.
- They would ask for God's forgiveness, and He would give it.
- They would live righteously.
- God would restore Israel and help them prosper as they lived in faithfulness to Him.

H. **Micah's** ministry as a prophet lasted 35 years in both the northern and the southern kingdoms (735-700 BC), during the time of the southern kings Jotham, Ahaz and Hezekiah.
- Micah was from Judah.
- He ministered at the same time as Isaiah.
- He preached that God would judge His people for mistreating the poor (*Mic. 2*), and for their corruption (*Mic. 3*).
- He predicted a number of things:[20]
    - The fall of Samaria (*1:6-7*). This happened in 721 BC. As a result, the northern kingdom would be no more.
    - The Assyrian invasion of Judah (*1:9-16*). Although Assyria would approach the gates of Jerusalem, God would spare the city for another 115 years before Babylon conquered it.
    - The fall of Jerusalem and destruction of the temple (*3:12; 7:14*). Micah actually predicted that Jerusalem would become rubble, and plowed like an open field. The temple site would be overgrown with brush. This vision of Jerusalem would have been nearly impossible to imagine for the Jews of Micah's time.
    - The exile in Babylon (*4:10*). The period of exile was actually a part of God's plan to restore Israel. After terrible punishment and this predicted time away from Jerusalem, God would bring Israel back to the Promised Land of the covenant.
    - The return from captivity and future restoration of Israel (*4:1-8, 13; 7:11, 14*). This prophecy has some reference to the rebuilding of Jerusalem and its walls as a sign of God's blessing at the end of the 70-year exile. Yet it also says that God would gather His people from captivity and restore Jerusalem as the center of worship not only for His people, but also for the nations. Israel would be restored as a powerful nation fed by the wealth of those nations who had resisted her.
    - Christ's birth in Bethlehem (*5:2*). The Messiah of Judah, Who would lead Israel into the time of its complete restoration, would be born in Bethlehem.
        ▷ The Magi used this verse to find the infant Jesus (*Mat. 2:5-6*).
    - The future reign of Christ (*Mic. 2:12-13; 4:1, 7*). These predictions tell that Jesus will gather the faithful remnant of Israel as a shepherd gathers a flock and lead them into Jerusalem, where He will establish His millennial reign.

I. **Isaiah's** ministry as a prophet lasted 58 years in the southern kingdom (739-681 BC), during the reigns of Uzziah, Jotham, Ahaz, Hezekiah, and Manasseh.

NOTES

- Isaiah is known as "the Messianic Prophet." In the Old Testament, only the Psalms refer to Christ more than the book of Isaiah.
- Isaiah gave many prophecies that are familiar to God's people today. Two of them are often mentioned as we celebrate Jesus' birth. They reveal a great deal about Jesus' birth and His character.
  - ▶ God told Isaiah to give King Ahaz a sign about God's faithfulness (*7:3*). God gave Isaiah the sign of the child Immanuel (*7:14-15*):

Therefore the Lord Himself will give you a sign: Behold, the virgin shall conceive and bear a Son, and shall call His name Immanuel. Curds and honey He shall eat, that He may know to refuse the evil and choose the good.

  - ▷ There are six things to note about the sign of Immanuel:
    - ◆ God Himself would give the sign.
    - ◆ The sign was for the entire house of David and not just King Ahaz.
    - ◆ The sign would be miraculous.
    - ◆ The sign involved a virgin birth (see *Mat. 1:22-23*).
    - ◆ The miracle would be "God with us," which is the literal meaning of the name "Immanuel." In other words, God would take on a human body.
    - ◆ The miraculous, divine child would also be completely human. He would eat what other children ate, and grow to human maturity as they did.

For unto us a Child is born, unto us a Son is given; and the government will be upon His shoulder. And His name will be called Wonderful, Counselor, Mighty God, Everlasting Father, Prince of Peace (*Isa. 9:6*).

  - → The phrase "a child is born" refers to Jesus' humanity or humanness (see *Luk. 2:7; Heb. 2:14; 1 Joh. 4:9*).
  - → The phrase "a son is given" refers to His deity (*Joh. 3:16*).
  - → The name "Wonderful" refers to His personality and character.
  - → The name "Counselor" refers of His knowledge of all things (see *Rom. 11:34; Joh. 2:24-25*).
  - → The name "Mighty God" refers to His strength and power as the only Son of the living God.
  - → The name "Everlasting Father" is literally "Father of Eternity" and refers to His role in creating the universe (see *Joh. 1:3; Col. 1:16; Heb. 1:2*).
  - → The name "Prince of Peace" refers to His unique status as God and man, which makes Him able to reconcile man with God.

Question:

Which of Isaiah's prophecies regarding Jesus is most important to you, and why? Use Scripture to back up your answer.

There are many prophecies about Christ from Isaiah. Several such prophecies are listed in the chart below:

Christ in Isaiah[21]

Event	Reference in the Book of Isaiah
Jesus Becoming Man	*7:14-15; 9:6*
Jesus' Youth in Nazareth	*11:1-2; 53:2; 7:15*
Jesus' Relationship with the Father	*42:1; 50:4-5*
Jesus' Miracles	*35:5-6*
Jesus' Message	*61:1-2*
Jesus' Specific Ministry to the Gentiles	*9:1-2*
Jesus' Gracious Ministry to All	*42:2-3*
Jesus' Suffering and Death	*50:6; 52:14; 53:1-10*
Jesus' Resurrection, Ascension, and Exaltation	*52:13; 53:10-12*
Jesus' Millennial Reign	*9:7; 42:4-7; 59:16-21; 11:3-5; 49:1-12; 32:1; 33:22*

Isaiah is quoted more times in the New Testament than any other Old Testament prophet. See the chart below for several examples:

Isaiah Quoted in the New Testament[22]

In reference to:	New Testament passage quoting Isaiah:
The ministry of John the Baptist	*Mat. 3:3; Luk. 3:4; Joh. 1:23*
Christ's ministry to the Gentiles	*Mat. 4:14-15; 12:17-18*
Christ's future rule over the Gentiles	*Rom. 15:12*
Christ's healing ministry	*Mat. 8:17*
Israel's blindness	*Mat. 13:14; Act. 28:25-27*
Israel's hypocrisy	*Mat. 15:7*
Israel's disobedience	*Rom. 10:16, 20*
Israel's saved remnant	*Rom. 9:27, 29*
Christ's sufferings	*Act. 8:28, 30*
Christ's anointing	*Luk. 4:17*

NOTES

- Isaiah's message may be divided into three sections, each telling about a different servant of God.
  - The first section is about Israel, God's faithless servant, and her enemies (*Isa. 1-35*).
  - The second section is about King Hezekiah, God's anxious servant (*Isa. 36-39*).
  - The third section is about Christ, God's faithful servant (*Isa. 40-66*).
- Isaiah was called to minister through a vision of God in the temple (*Isa. 6:1-6*).
- The vision helped Isaiah better understand two things:
  - God's holiness.
  - His own sinfulness.
- The fact that God would still use Isaiah to serve Him humbled Isaiah.
- Isaiah understood that God's character demanded sincere worship and service. Making sacrifices without true worship would not satisfy the living God (see *Rom. 12:1-2*).
- Isaiah predicted many things. These predictions came to pass during Isaiah's lifetime. They showed that Isaiah was a true prophet who spoke the truth of God:
  - Judah's salvation from the possible Syrian and Israelite invasion (*7:4, 16*).
  - Assyria's domination of Syria and Israel (*8:4; 17:1-14; 28:1-4*).
  - Assyria's invasion of Judah (*8:7-8*).
    - Jerusalem would be saved during this invasion (*37:33-35*).
  - The Assyrians would judge Moab within three years (*15-16*).
  - The Assyrians would conquer Egypt and Ethiopia (*18-20*).
  - Arabia would be destroyed (*21:13-17*).
  - Tyre would be destroyed (*23:1-12*).
  - Hezekiah's life would be extended by 15 years (*38:5*).
  - God's judgment on Assyria (*10:5-34; 14:24-27; 30:27-33; 37:36*).
- The following predictions came to pass after Isaiah's lifetime. They showed that God gave Isaiah prophecies not just for his day, but also for future generations. For example, the prophecies about Babylon gave the Jewish exiles hope while they were in captivity there:
  - The Babylonian captivity (*3:1-8; 5:26-30; 22:1-14; 39:5-7*).
  - The overthrow of Babylon by Cyrus (*13:17-22; 14:1-23; 21:2; 46:11; 48:14*).
  - The ongoing emptiness of Babylon (*13:20-22; 47:1-15*).
  - Conquests of Cyrus the Persian (*41:2-3; 44:28; 45:1-4*).
  - Cyrus' decree that returned the exiles to Jerusalem (*44:38; 45:13*).
  - The joy of the returning exiles (*48:20*).
  - The restoration of Tyre (*23:13-18*).
  - The ministry of John the Baptist (*40:3-5*).
- Many scholars believe that Isaiah was executed at the order of the evil king Manasseh.
- The insights God gave Isaiah regarding His character, the Person of Jesus Christ, and the need to honor God with a sincere heart apply as much today as they did in Isaiah's time.

J. **Nahum** prophesied for 30 years in the southern kingdom (650-620 BC), during the reigns of Manasseh, Amon, and Josiah. His single message was the destruction of Nineveh.

K. **Zephaniah's** prophetic ministry lasted 20 years in the southern kingdom (640-620 BC), during the reign of Josiah. His message was simple: the Day of the Lord is coming with judgment on all who mistreat the poor and dishonor God.

L. **Habakkuk's** ministry lasted three years in the southern kingdom (609-606 BC), during the reigns of Jehoahaz and Jehoiakim.
- Habakkuk asked two questions of God and received two answers (*Hab. 1-2*).
    ▶ The first question was: "Why do wicked people around me in Judah seem to prosper?" The prophet was bothered that God seemed to be allowing evil in Judah (*1:3-4*). Worse, the prophet thought that God was doing nothing about it.
        ▷ God's answer was: "Babylon is about to punish the wicked people in Judah." Babylon would become a feared force in the region we now know as the Middle East (*1:5-8*). God was about to bring the evil in Judah to an end.
    ▶ The second question was: "Why use Babylon when Babylon is more wicked than Judah?" Habakkuk could not understand why God would allow an unrighteous nation like Babylon to punish His people.
        ▷ God's answer was: "Live by faith that I will always do what is right." God would punish Babylon, but in His timing (*2:3*).
- Habakkuk states, *"The just shall live by faith"* (*2:4*). This verse is quoted three times in the New Testament (*Rom. 1:17; Gal. 3:11; Heb. 10:38*).
    ▶ Even today, sometimes it seems that God's ways don't make sense. At those times, we must respond in faith and trust that God is doing the right thing for His glory and our good.

M. **Jeremiah** prophesied for 52 years in the southern kingdom (627-575 BC), under Judah's kings Josiah, Jehoiakim, Jehoiachin, Zedekiah, and the Babylonian rulers Nebuchadnezzar, Gedaliah, and Johanan.
- Jeremiah entered his prophetic ministry during the reign of Josiah (*Jer. 1:1-10*). He tried to use his youth as an excuse for not becoming God's prophet, but God told Jeremiah that He had chosen him for the task. God also told Jeremiah that He would give the young prophet the words to say as he spoke.
- Jeremiah boldly spoke God's message of judgment on Judah. As a result he was persecuted by his own family (*12:6*), the people of his hometown Anathoth (*11:21*), and finally all of Judah.
    ▶ God showed him an almond tree rod at the beginning of his ministry. The almond tree flowered earlier than other trees. It was a sign that God would fulfill His judgment soon (*1:11*).
    ▶ Jeremiah also saw a pot of boiling water that was tipping from the north to the south. This was a sign of the coming Babylonian attack (*1:13*).

NOTES

NOTES

- Eighteen years after his ministry began, Jeremiah stood weeping at the funeral of King Josiah (*2 Chr. 35:25*). He knew that Josiah's death probably meant the quick decay of Judah's spiritual life.
- Jeremiah warned the majority of people in Judah about the coming Babylonian captivity (*Jer. 2-45*).
  - ▶ Jeremiah listed Judah's sins:
    - ▷ They had turned their backs on God, the fountain of living waters (*2:13*; see *Joh. 4:14*).
    - ▷ Judah had become evil (*2:21*).
    - ▷ No amount of soap would cleanse them (*2:22*).
    - ▷ Judah's leaders were stained with the blood of the innocent and poor (*2:34*).
    - ▷ They had committed spiritual adultery without shame (*3:3*).
    - ▷ They worshiped false gods whenever they could (*3:6*).
    - ▷ They had killed God's prophets (*2:30*).
    - ▷ They were hard-hearted rebels (*6:28*).
    - ▷ They had worshiped idols in the temple itself (*7:18; 44:17*).
    - ▷ They had sacrificed their children as burnt offerings to evil and false gods (*7:31; 19:5*).
  - ▶ Yet Jeremiah also gave Judah God's invitation to return to Him (*3:12-14; 26:1-7*).
    - ▷ Judah could still escape judgment by cleansing their hearts and purifying their thoughts (*4:14*).
    - ▷ This invitation to draw near to God through pure thinking and living is given again in *James 4:8*.
    - ▷ If Judah repented they could remain in the land (*7:3*). If Judah did not repent a great darkness would cover them (*13:16*).
  - ▶ Jeremiah warned Judah about the consequences they would face in disobeying God.
    - ▷ The depth of Judah's suffering would surprise the Gentile nations around them (*19:8; 22:8; 25:11*).
    - ▷ Not even Assyria or Egypt would be able to help Judah against Babylon (*2:18, 36*).
    - ▷ The temple would be destroyed (*7:14*).
    - ▷ Judah's people would run from their cities (*4:5-7*) as enemy soldiers moved among them like deadly snakes (*8:17*).
    - ▷ Many would die by the sword (*15:3*), disease (*16:3-4*), and starvation (*21:9*).
    - ▷ Bodies that were not buried would cover the valleys outside Jerusalem, becoming food for wild birds and animals (*7:32-33; 9:22; 12:8-9*).
    - ▷ Babylon would carry thousands of Judeans into captivity for a period of 70 years (*7:15; 25:11; 29:10*).
  - ▶ Despite Jeremiah's warnings, Judah rejected his message. This caused Jeremiah great sadness, causing him to weep again and again over Judah's rebellion and coming judgment (*4:19; 8:21; 9:1-2, 10; 13:17; 14:17*).

▷ Jeremiah was faithful to the message of judgment God had given him. As stated earlier, this caused him to be persecuted in many ways.
- ❖ The chief temple priest, Pashur, had Jeremiah whipped and put in stocks (*20:1-3*).
- ❖ A mob of priests and prophets nearly killed Jeremiah after he spoke a message of judgment against them and Jerusalem (*26:7-9*).
- ❖ Jeremiah also suffered at the hands of the wicked kings Jehoiakim (*28:21-24; 36:21-26*) and Zedekiah (see *21:3-7; 34:1-5; 37:11-38:28*).
- ❖ One of the most important things in Jeremiah's prophecies is the New Covenant, described in *31:31-14*:

Behold, the days are coming, says the LORD, when I will make a new covenant with the house of Israel and with the house of Judah-not according to the covenant that I made with their fathers in the day that I took them by the hand to lead them out of the land of Egypt, My covenant which they broke, though I was a husband to them, says the LORD. But this is the covenant that I will make with the house of Israel after those days, says the LORD: I will put My law in their minds, and write it on their hearts; and I will be their God, and they shall be My people. No more shall every man teach his neighbor, and every man his brother, saying, "Know the LORD," for they all shall know Me, from the least of them to the greatest of them, says the LORD. For I will forgive their iniquity, and their sin I will remember no more.

▶ This New Covenant would include the entire house of Israel.
▶ This New Covenant would be different than the covenant of Moses.
▶ The New Covenant would go into effect at the start of the millennium, "after those days" (*31:33*) and after "the time of Jacob's trouble" (*30:7*).
▶ The New Covenant will be both unconditional and everlasting (*31:37*; see *33:20-26*).
▶ The Son of David is the Mediator of the New Covenant (*33:15-18; 30:9*).
- Jeremiah also pronounced judgment on nine Gentile nations in the area (*46-51*).
- Jeremiah predicted many things. Some of them are:
  ▶ The fall of Jerusalem (*1:14-16; 4:5-9; 6:1-6; 32:2, 3; 38:17, 18*).
  ▶ The destruction of the temple (*7:11-15; 26:6-9*).
  ▶ Babylon's occupation of Egypt (*43:9-13*).
  ▶ Seventy-year captivity of Judah in Babylon (*25:11; 29:10*).
  ▶ Return to Jerusalem after the captivity (*27:19-22; 30:3, 10-11, 18-21; 33:3-9*).
  ▶ Defeat of Babylon (*25:12; 27:7*).
  ▶ Herod's slaughter of the innocents at Bethlehem (*31:15-16*; see *Mat. 2:18*).

NOTES

NOTES

- ▸ Final restoration of Israel (*30:18-21; 31:38, 39; 33:7-9*).
- Jeremiah also wrote the book of Lamentations. The book mourns the destruction of Jerusalem in 586 BC.
- It talks about a city in rubble and people who have seen their friends, neighbors and family members slaughtered or carried off to a foreign land.
  - ▸ It would have been easy for Jeremiah and the Jews to lose all hope. But in *Lamentations 3:21-31*, Jeremiah remembers that God will not cast off His people forever:

This I recall to my mind, therefore I have hope. Through the LORD's mercies we are not consumed, because His compassions fail not. They are new every morning; great is Your faithfulness. "The LORD is my portion" says my soul, "Therefore I hope in Him!" The LORD is good to those who wait for Him, to the soul who seeks Him. It is good that one should hope and wait quietly for the salvation of the LORD. It is good for a man to bear the yoke in his youth. Let him sit alone and keep silent, because God has laid it on him; Let him put his mouth in the dust-There may yet be hope. Let him give his cheek to the one who strikes him, and be full of reproach. For the Lord will not cast off forever.

Questions:

Find three events from the Chaotic Stage that demonstrates the disorder in Israel, Judah, or both kingdoms. Write the places in the Bible where you found the events.

1)

2)

3)

Find three events from the Chaotic Stage that show God's care for His people. Write the places in the Bible where you found these events.

1)

2)

3)

What do you see your people needing in the new church regarding the truths of the Chaotic Kingdom?

Chapter Eight
The Captivity Stage

1. Captivity Stage Overview

A. The Captivity Stage covers the time from 605-538 BC, and the books of Ezekiel and Daniel.
- This stage begins with the capture of the southern kingdom (Judah) by the Babylonians, and ends with the decree of Cyrus allowing the return of the exiles from Babylon to Jerusalem.
- *Psalm 137* describes the beginning of this stage, and *Psalm 126* describes the end.

B. The key people in the Captivity Stage are: Daniel, Nebuchadnezzar, Shadrach, Meshach, Abednego, Belshazzar, Darius, and Ezekiel.

C. The key events in the Captivity Stage are: the personal deliverance of Daniel and his friends, the destruction of the first temple, the description of the future millennial temple, an overview of the Gentile world powers, a preview of Israel's future, and the fall of Babylon.

D. The locations of the key events in this stage are:
- Personal deliverance of Daniel and his friends: Babylon.
- Destruction of the first temple: Jerusalem.
- Description of the future millennial temple: *Ezekiel 40-48*.
- Overview of Gentile world powers: *Daniel 7-8*.
- Preview of Israel's future: *Ezekiel 36-37*.

E. There are other important things in this stage:
- The writing of two eyewitness accounts of captivity in Babylon. One is from Daniel, the other from Ezekiel.
  ▶ As other books of the Bible, these accounts mention places, events and people that show the Bible is a historical book.
- References to the archangels Gabriel and Michael and their activity (*Dan. 8, 12*).
  ▶ These references tell about what angels do as they serve God, and reveal that God often has them work on behalf of His people.
- The only description of God the Father in the Bible (*Dan. 7:9-14*).
  ▶ This vision of a majestic God was mentioned again in *Revelation 1:9-20*, and applied to Jesus Christ to show that Jesus is God.

2. The Bible Account of the Captivity Stage

A. **Ezekiel** (593-560 BC).
- Ezekiel was a priest and prophet. He was also the son of a priest. He was taken to Babylon in 597 BC with Jehoiachin.

- ▶ Ezekiel began his ministry at the age of 30. He lived in Babylon on the Chebar, a canal that flowed from the Euphrates River (*Eze. 1:1-3*).
- ▶ Ezekiel reminded the captives in Babylon of their sin (*Eze. 4-24*). He also told them to look forward to God's future blessings (*Eze. 33-48*).
- ▶ God called Ezekiel to be Israel's watchman in Babylon (*Eze. 3*).
- False prophets told the Jews in Jerusalem and Babylon that God would not destroy Jerusalem. However, God had told Ezekiel that He would. Ezekiel attempted to tell the truth through symbols, parables, visions and messages that Jerusalem would be destroyed (*Eze. 4-24*).
  - ▶ Ezekiel performed twelve symbolic acts.
    - ▷ He drew a map of Jerusalem with enemy camps and weapons in place. Then he placed an iron plate between the map and himself (*Eze. 4:1-3*).
      - ◆ This showed the Babylonian army was immovable, and escape from Jerusalem would be impossible.
    - ▷ He lay on his left side for 390 days to stand for the sin of the northern kingdom. Each day stood for one year in the kingdom (*Eze. 4:4-5*).
    - ▷ Ezekiel then lay on his right side for 40 days to stand for the sin of the southern kingdom. Again, each day stood for a year in the kingdom (*Eze. 4:6*).
      - ◆ The total number of years (430) stood for the punishment of exile and Gentile rule. If the exile in Babylon began in 597 BC this punishment would end around 167 BC. At that time the Jews regained their rule through the Maccabean revolt.[23]
    - ▷ The prophet made bread from mixed grains and baked it over dried cow dung (*Eze. 4:9-17*).
      - ◆ This showed that there was little food in Jerusalem.
    - ▷ Ezekiel shaved his head and beard with a sword. He divided the hair into three equal parts. He burned one third of the hair. He cut up another third with the sword. He scattered the final third in the wind (*Eze. 5:1-4*).
      - ◆ This showed what was coming to Judah and Jerusalem. One third of the people would die by fire. Another third would die by the sword. The remaining third would scatter.
    - ▷ He clapped his hands and stamped his feet to gain attention (*Eze. 6:11*).
    - ▷ Ezekiel set just a few pieces of baggage outside his home. Then he dug an entrance through the city wall. He went through the entrance covering his face (*Eze. 12:1-16*).
      - ◆ The baggage represented the hurried way the exiles would leave their homes.
      - ◆ The entrance in the wall represented their need to leave Jerusalem.
      - ◆ The covered face represented Zedekiah, Judah's last king who had been blinded for his rebellion and taken captive in to Babylon.
    - ▷ He trembled as he ate his food and rationed out his water as if there would be no more (*Eze. 12:17-20*).

NOTES

- ▷ Ezekiel slashed the air with a gleaming sword, and cried out as he beat his thigh (*Eze. 21:9-17*).
- ▷ The prophet drew a map with two routes for the King of Babylon to follow. One led to Jerusalem and the other to Rabbath-Ammon. Both cities had rebelled against Babylon (*Eze. 21:21, 22*).
- ▷ Ezekiel filled a pot with choice meats and boiled it until the meat fell off the bones. He then dumped the pot's contents and waited for the pot to bake itself dry, removing all the rust and scum (*Eze. 24:1-14*).
  - ◆ This meant the judgment fire of God would consume everyone, even the rich and noble, in Jerusalem. No one would be allowed to stay in the land so it could be fully cleansed of moral filth.
- ▷ God told Ezekiel not to show any outward sadness over the death of his wife (*Eze. 24:15-18*).
  - ◆ This showed that God would not mourn over the death of Jerusalem.

Questions:

What do you think the most difficult part of Ezekiel's ministry as a prophet would have been? Discuss.

- ▶ Ezekiel delivered twelve judgment messages. These were their main points.
  - ▷ God had held back His judgment in spite of Israel's disobedience (*Eze. 20:7-10, 14, 21-22*).
  - ▷ God took no joy in judging His people and still called for them to repent (*Eze. 18:3-32*).
  - ▷ Because Judah did not listen to God, they would soon be judged (*Eze. 7:6, 12*).
  - ▷ Judah would be destroyed because of the sin of the present generation, not because of their fathers' sin (*Eze. 18:1-4, 20*).
  - ▷ Even the presence of godly men like Noah, Daniel and Job would not stop God's judgment of Jerusalem (*Eze. 14:14, 20*).
  - ▷ Jerusalem's armies would not be able to defend the city (*Eze. 7:14*).
  - ▷ Jerusalem's wealth would do no good in preventing its destruction (*Eze. 7:19*).
  - ▷ The city that once belonged to God had become Satan's city.
  - ▷ God would bring the worst nations and people to Judah to occupy His people's homes (*Eze. 7:24*).

- ▷ Judah's cities and idols would be destroyed (*Eze. 6:4, 6*).
- ▷ War, famine, wild beasts, and plagues would come to Judah's citizens (*Eze. 14:21*).
- ▶ Ezekiel also told six parables.
    - ▷ One of the parables described a fruitless vine tree that was burned because it refused to do the single thing it was created to do: bear fruit (*Eze. 15:1-8*).
        - ◆ The vine stood for Israel.

Question:

How is the vine Ezekiel tells about in *Ezekiel 15:1-8* like the vine Jesus mentions in *John 15:1-8*? How are the two vines different? Use Scripture to support your answers.

How can Ezekiel's example help you as a new Church Planter? Discuss.

- ▶ For their hostility toward God and His people, Ezekiel spoke judgment on nations and cities.
    - ▷ Ammon took joy in Jerusalem's destruction and captivity (*Lam. 2:15*). As a result, Ammon would be taken over by desert tribes. Its capital city would become a camel pasture (*Eze. 25:1-7*).
    - ▷ Moab treated God like any other local idol. As a result, the same tribes that took over Ammon also took over Moab's cities (*Eze. 25:8-11*).
    - ▷ Tyre also took joy in the fall of Judah to Babylon (*Eze. 26:2*). They had a history of selling Jews as slaves (*Joe. 3:4-8; Amo. 1:9-10*).
        - ◆ Tyre was the greatest commercial city in Old Testament times.
        - ◆ Tyre was two cities together. One was on the Mediterranean, and the other was on an island about a mile away.
        - ◆ God's judgment on Tyre was that both locations would be destroyed and never rebuilt (*Eze. 26-28*).
- ▶ Ezekiel then spoke about the difference between false shepherds and the only true Shepherd, Jesus Christ (*Eze. 34*).
    - ▷ False shepherds feed and care for themselves, not their sheep (*Eze. 34:2-10; 16*).

NOTES

▷ The Great Shepherd is the best protection for the sheep (*Eze. 34:11-28*).
  • He searches out the lost.
  • He delivers them from their enemies.
  • He gathers them from all nations.
  • He feeds them on the mountains of Israel.
  • He gives them green pastures.
  • He binds their wounds.
  • He heals the sick.
  • He promises their safety.

Question:

Look again at *Ezekiel 34*. What makes it easy for someone to be a false shepherd today? Discuss.

▶ God removed Israel out of the Promised Land because of their sin. Ezekiel told the exiles that God's plan was to restore the nation of Israel (*Eze. 36, 37*).
  ▷ Israel needed restoration for two reasons.
    • To punish Israel's enemies.
    • To honor God's name.
  ▷ Ezekiel's vision of this restoration featured dry bones. The vision began with Ezekiel speaking to a valley filled with dry bones of Israel's people.
    • The bones join together and become covered with flesh. Ezekiel speaks again and life enters the bodies, which form a huge army.
  ▷ God led Ezekiel to create a symbol of the restored Israel.
    • The prophet carves the name "Judah" on one stick, and "Ephraim" (Israel) on another. He holds the two sticks together. This showed that God would bring all twelve tribes together again.

Questions:

Choose two or three words that you think best describe God's restoration of Israel as told in *Ezekiel 36-37*. Use Scripture to support your answers.

What results show that God has restored a person? Discuss.

- Ezekiel then told about a latter day's invasion of Palestine by an evil nation from the north (*Eze. 38-39*).
- Ezekiel then describes the millennial temple (*Eze. 40-48*).[24]
- Although God spoke judgment through Ezekiel, He also promised Jerusalem's final restoration. This promise was great comfort to the exiles along the Chebar and in Jerusalem.

B. **Daniel** (605-536 BC).
- As a teenager, Daniel was taken captive by Nebuchadnezzar. This was in the first Babylonian assault on Jerusalem in 605 BC. In Babylon, Daniel lived without compromising his faith in God or God's standards for living. He served with excellence under three kings: Nebuchadnezzar, Belshazzar, and Darius.
  - ▶ Daniel was known for his wisdom and righteousness (*Eze. 28:3; 14:14*).
  - ▶ Daniel was also known for his ability to interpret dreams (*Dan. 2:24; 4:19*).
- Daniel's first test of faith in Babylon was whether or not to eat food from the king's table. As a court official in training, Daniel and his friends could eat the rich foods from the king's table. Yet, eating many of those foods meant breaking God's laws about diet. Daniel and his friends decided not to eat the king's food (*Dan. 1*).
  - ▶ When the king's steward said they might grow weak without the king's food, Daniel asked for a ten-day test.
    - ▷ During the test, Daniel and his friends would eat only vegetables and water.
    - ▷ At the end of the test, Daniel and his friends looked healthier than those who had eaten from the king's table.
    - ▷ At the end of their training, Daniel and his friends had ten times the wisdom and understanding than the king's magicians and astrologers.
- Nebuchadnezzar had a troubling dream and asked his court officials to tell him not only what the dream meant, but also what the dream was. The king's officials could not tell him, and were sentenced to death. Before they were killed, Daniel asked a king's servant to ask the king for time to interpret the dream (*Dan. 2*).
  - ▶ God revealed the dream to Daniel that night.
  - ▶ Daniel explained the dream to the king.
    - ▷ The king had seen a huge statue of a man.
      - ◆ Its head was gold.
      - ◆ Its chest and arms were silver.
      - ◆ Its belly and thighs were brass.
      - ◆ Its legs were iron and its feet part iron and clay.

- ▷ A rock fell on the statue and turned it into powder.
- ▷ The rock grew until it filled the earth.
- ▷ The statue stood for four Gentile nations of power.
  - ◆ The golden head was Babylon (which dominated the known world from 606-539 BC).
  - ◆ The silver chest and arms were Persia (which defeated Babylon and ruled the known world from 539-331 BC).
  - ◆ The brass belly and thighs were Greece (which defeated Persia and then dominated the world from 331-323 BC).
  - ◆ The iron legs and iron and clay feet were Rome (which defeated Greece and became the world power from 322 BC-AD 476).
- ▷ In the days of the final world power, God would crush every earthly kingdom through His Rock (Jesus Christ) and set up an eternal kingdom.
- ▷ Nebuchadnezzar fell down and worshiped Daniel when he heard the interpretation. He then promoted Daniel and his friends.

- King Nebuchadnezzar made a 27-meter golden image of himself. He set up the image on the plains of Dura in Babylon. He commanded that all his officials bow down and worship it when the trumpets sounded. This would show the king's importance, and also make him the central figure in Babylon (*Dan. 2-3*).
  - ▶ The Hebrew officials Shadrach, Meshach, and Abednego would not bow down and worship the idol.
    - ▷ Nebuchadnezzar ordered them to be thrown into a fiery furnace. The heat from the furnace consumed the guards bringing the three Hebrews to its edge.
    - ▷ When Shadrach, Meshach and Abednego were in the furnace, a fourth man joined them. The Son of God delivers them from the furnace unhurt.
    - ▷ The king changed his order about bowing to the idol. He also promoted Shadrach, Meshach and Abednego.

Question:

In the first few chapters of *Daniel*, it is clear that God rewards those who remain faithful to Him and His ways. What are some ways God has rewarded you as you have served Him? Discuss.

- Nebuchadnezzar had another dream of a mighty and beautiful tree that everyone could see. It provided fruit for the whole world, and shade and protection for the animals and birds. A heavenly figure came and ordered the tree cut down and its fruit scattered. The tree's stump was all that was left. It had a band of iron and brass around it (*Dan. 4*).

- ▶ The tree that fell stood for a man who would be given the mind of an animal for seven years.
- ▶ The tree was cut down so everyone would know that the Most High rules the kingdom of men, giving it to whomever He wants.
- ▶ Daniel interpreted the dream for Nebuchadnezzar.
  - ▷ The tree stood for Nebuchadnezzar.
  - ▷ The heavenly visitor was an angel of the Most High.
  - ▷ The destruction of the tree was not total. The band around the trunk meant that the tree might grow again. God could still have a purpose for Nebuchadnezzar.
  - ▷ Yet, Nebuchadnezzar would still go through seven years with the mind of an animal. He would only be restored when he humbled himself.
- ▶ Nebuchadnezzar still spoke proudly of his accomplishments. A year after this dream, he became insane as his dream had described.
  - ▷ The king thought and lived like an animal for seven years. He was restored when he humbled himself and glorified God.
- Belshazzar, who ruled Babylon together with his father, gave a feast for his top 1000 officers. As the night went on, Belshazzar ordered that the gold and silver cups from the Jerusalem temple be brought to the feast so the guests could use them to drink and honor the Babylonian gods. In the middle of a toast, a floating hand is seen writing on the wall next to the king's table. He cries for help, but those around him can do nothing (*Dan. 5*).
  - ▶ Belshazzar finally calls for Daniel.
    - ▷ He offers the third highest position in Babylon to Daniel if Daniel interprets the writing on the wall.
  - ▶ Daniel begins by reminding Belshazzar that pride nearly destroyed his grandfather Nebuchadnezzar. But Nebuchadnezzar had turned to God after his seven years of insanity.
  - ▶ Daniel interprets that the writing had three messages from God to Belshazzar.
    - ▷ The first word, "Mene," meant that God had numbered the days of Babylon and those days were coming to an end.
    - ▷ "Tekel" meant that God had measured Belshazzar according to His standards, and Belshazzar had not met God's standards.
    - ▷ "Upharsin" meant that Babylon was divided and given to the Medes and Persians.
  - ▶ That night Belshazzar was killed, and Darius the Mede took over as the ruler in Babylon.
- Daniel was one of three presidents Darius appointed to supervise the 129 governors in Babylon. Daniel was doing his job so well that Darius was thinking about promoting Daniel above the other two presidents. The other officials plotted against Daniel. They tricked Darius into signing an order that made it against the law to pray to anyone but Darius for thirty days (*Dan. 6*).
  - ▶ Almost immediately, Daniel was found praying to God.
  - ▶ Daniel's punishment was to be put into a den of lions.
    - ▷ God shut the lions' mouths and Daniel survived.

NOTES

- ▶ Darius ordered all the citizens to consider the God of Daniel.
- ▶ Darius also ordered those who tricked him and their families to be put into the lions' den. They were quickly killed by the lions.

Questions:

What did you learn from Daniel's example of faithfulness in *Daniel 6*? Discuss.

From what you read in *Daniel 6*, how does God help His people in times of persecution or danger? Discuss.

- Daniel had a vision that told about godless kingdoms and God's Kingdom. The godless kingdoms are the same four that Nebuchadnezzar had seen in his dream (see *Dan. 2*). In this vision, Daniel sees four beasts coming out of an ocean (*Dan. 7*).
- Daniel had another vision. This vision involved horns that represented Gentile nations and their leaders (*Dan. 8*).
- During the first year of Persian rule (538 BC), Daniel was reading from the book of Jeremiah. He was reminded that God had determined Jerusalem must lie in ruins for 70 years (see *Jer. 25:11; 29:10*). Daniel prayed with a humble heart. He remembered God's promises and mercy (*Dan. 9*).
  - ▶ Daniel confessed both national sins and his own. As he prayed, he also asked:
    - ▷ That God would bring His people out of Babylon as He brought them out of Egypt.
    - ▷ That God would forgive.
    - ▷ That God would permit the temple to be built again in Jerusalem.
- Daniel was on the banks of the Tigris River. He had been fasting and praying for three weeks. He may have been in sorrow for several reasons. It might have been the sins of his people, or the suffering his people were facing. It could have been that so few of the exiles decided to go back to Jerusalem. Whatever the reason Daniel was deep in prayer (*Dan. 10*).
- Daniel then had a prophecy about unrighteous rulers.
  - ▶ Daniel also warned that the antichrist (*Dan. 11:36-45*).
    - ▷ He would be totally self-willed.
    - ▷ He would lift up himself and put down God.
    - ▷ He would prosper, but only for a while.
    - ▷ He would not honor the gods of his fathers.
    - ▷ He would have no desire for women.

- ▷ He would honor the god of the fortress.
- ▷ He would be attacked by two southern and northern kings.
- ▷ He would occupy the Holy Land and Egypt.
- ▷ He would hear frightening news in Egypt.
- ▷ He would return to the Holy Land to wage war.
- ▷ He would be destroyed by Christ on Mt. Zion.[25]
- Daniel's visions as recorded in the book of Daniel finish with a further look at the end times.
- Although God revealed many things to Daniel in this prophetic chapter, it is important to see that Daniel "did not understand" everything he heard (*12:8*). Yet Daniel trusted God both for the prophecy He gave and for the future results that would restore both His creation and His people at the end of history.

Questions:

Find three promises from God that you think might have been the most encouraging to the exiles of the Captivity Stage. Write the place where you found each promise in the Bible next to the promise itself.

1)

2)

3)

Find three promises from God made during the Captivity Stage that encourage you. Write the place where you found each promise in the Bible next to the promise itself.

1)

2)

3)

Chapter Nine
The Return Stage

1. Return Stage Overview

A. The Return Stage covers the time from 538-400 BC, and the books of Ezra, Esther, Nehemiah, Haggai, Zechariah, and Malachi.
   - This stage begins with Cyrus' decree allowing the return of the exiles from Babylon to Jerusalem, and ends with the ministry of the prophet Malachi in Jerusalem.

B. The key people in the Return Stage are: Cyrus, Joshua, Zerubabel, Ezra, Ahasuerus, Esther, Mordecai, Haman, Nehemiah, and Atraxerxes.

C. The key events in the Return Stage are: the decree of Cyrus, the construction of the second temple, the rebuilding of the walls, and the deliverance of the Jews in Persia.

D. The locations of the key events in this stage are:
   - The decree of Cyrus: Persia, perhaps from Cyrus' capital Pasargadae.
   - Construction of the second temple: Jerusalem.
   - Rebuilding of the walls: Jerusalem.
   - Deliverance of the Jews in Persia: the Persian city of Shushan.[26]

E. There are other important things in this stage.
   - Persia, under Cyrus the Great, conquered Babylon (about 539 BC).
   - The restoration of the Feast of Tabernacles (*Neh. 2:21-23*).
   - The first Feast of Purim (*Est. 9-10*).

2. The Bible Account of the Return Stage

The Bible and history form a chronology of the Return Stage that is recorded on the following chart.[27]

The Return Stage Order of Events

Foreign King	Date (BC)	Event	Scripture
Cyrus the Great	539-530	Conquers Babylon	*Daniel 5*
		Decrees return	*Ezra 1-3*
Canbyses	530-522	No OT reference	--
Smerdis	522-520	Stops temple work	*Ezra 4:1-23*
Darius the Great	520-486	Orders work to continue	*Ezra 4:24; 6:1-22*
Ahasuerus	486-465	Makes Esther his queen	*Esther 1-10*
Artaxerxes	465-424	Allows Ezra to return	*Ezra 7-12*
		Allows Nehemiah to return	*Nehemiah 1-13*

There were three trips of the exiles from Jerusalem to Babylon. They are listed on the chart that follows.[28]

From Jerusalem to Babylon

Date	Captives	Prophets	Foreign Kings
606 BC	Daniel	(In Babylon) Daniel	(Before 539 BC) Nebuchadnezzar
597 BC	Ezekiel	(In Babylon) Ezekiel	(Before 539 BC) Belshazzar
586 BC	Zedekiah	(In Jerusalem) Jeremiah	(After 539 BC) Cyrus and Darius

There were also three return trips of the exiles from Babylon to Jerusalem. They are listed below.[29]

From Babylon to Jerusalem

Date	Leader	Foreign King	Old Testament Prophet
536 BC	Zerubbabel and Joshua	Cyrus the Great Cambyses Smerdis Darius the Great	Haggai Zechariah
455 BC	Ezra	Artaxerxes	Ezra
445 BC	Nehemiah	Artaxerxes	Nehemiah

A. **Ezra's** account of Zerubbabel and the first returning exiles (536 BC).
- Zerubbabel led the first wave of exiles from Babylon to Jerusalem in 536 BC (*Ezr. 1-6*). Ezra wrote down the story of Zerubbabel and Joshua, the high priest who helped him lead the exiles.
    - ▶ Cyrus' decree gave the opportunity for Jewish exiles to go back to Jerusalem.
        - ▷ Cyrus signed the return decree (*Ezr. 1:1-4*).
        - ▷ A spiritual Jewish minority responded (*Ezr. 1:5-11*). 40,000 exiles traveled back to Jerusalem.
    - ▶ The Jewish people reclaimed their spiritual home.
        - ▷ They reclaimed their family line (*Ezr. 2*), and their theology (*Ezr. 3*).
            - ◆ When they reached Jerusalem, they built the altar and kept the feasts.
    - ▶ The exiles went through lies and discouragement.
        - ▷ They were tempted to compromise (*Ezr. 4:1-3*).
        - ▷ Their enemies spread lies about them to try to stop the building of Jerusalem and the temple (*Ezr. 4:4-24*).
    - ▶ God sustains His people through the ministry of Haggai and Zechariah (*Ezr. 5:1; 6:14*).

NOTES

NOTES

B. **Haggai** (520 BC).
- Haggai had traveled back to Jerusalem from Babylon with Zerubbabel in 536 BC. Work on the temple stopped two years later. Darius of Persia sent out the orders that the exiles could build again with royal approval in about 522 BC. Haggai's job was to get all the exiles to build again.
  ▶ Haggai's first encouragement to the returned exiles was to do what they came to Jerusalem to do.
    ▷ They needed to continue with the task of building the temple (*Hag. 1:2-7*).
    ▷ They needed to go up on the mountain to get material for the Lord's house, not their own houses (*Hag. 1:8-11*).
    ▷ They needed to be passionate about the Lord (*Hag. 1:12-15*).
  ▶ Haggai's second encouragement to the returned exiles was to have patience.
    ▷ They needed patience in spite of the insignificant temple they had just built (*Hag. 2:1-5*).
    ▷ They needed patience to finish the magnificent temple they someday would build (*Hag. 2:6-9*).
  ▶ Haggai then gave the Jews these facts to think about as they continued building.
    ▷ The fact that Judah's contamination came from their wrong attitudes about rebuilding the temple (*Hag. 2:10-17*).
    ▷ God was determined to see the temple rebuilt. He was with them (*Hag. 2:18, 19*).
    ▷ The fact that the coming tribulation would show God's power to the nations (*Hag. 2:20-22*).
    ▷ The fact that Zerubbabel was God's chosen leader for this task (*Hag. 2:23*).

Questions:

Haggai ministered to a group of Jews who did not give God first place in their lives. Find two possible reasons these Jews no longer put God first. Support your answer with Scripture.

What things might cause us not to give God first place in our lives today, even though we are God's people?

C. **Zechariah** (520 BC).
- Zechariah joined Haggai in the role of prophet as the temple in Jerusalem was rebuilt. God's people were about to give up on the temple project. Zechariah shared his visions and parables of how God was working.
  ▶ Zechariah shared ten visions (*Zec. 1-6*).
    ▷ The rider on a red horse (*Zec. 1:7-17*).
      * An appearance of the Son of God and some angels watching over Jerusalem showed that God was watching over them.
    ▷ The four horns (*Zec. 1:18-19*).
      * This may represent the four Gentile world powers which scattered Israel. It showed that God knew the people's situation.
    ▷ The four artisans (*Zec. 1:20-21*).
      * This probably refers to the first four sealed judgments in *Revelation 6:1-8*. It shows that God is powerful, and that He will use His power to make things right.
    ▷ The man with the measuring line (*Zec. 2:1-13*).
      * This refers to the measuring of Jerusalem during the millennium (*Eze. 40:1-5; 48: 30-35*). It shows that God's plans for the future are ready.
    ▷ The confrontation in heaven (*Zec. 3:1-10*).
      * When Zechariah sees Joshua the high priest in his vision, Joshua is wearing dirty garments and standing before God.
        → Satan accuses Joshua for wearing dirty clothes before God.
      * Christ rebukes Satan, removes Joshua's dirty clothing, and replaces it with clean garments.
        → Joshua is free to serve God with his whole heart.
        → God promises the Branch (the Messiah), will cleanse the land as He cleansed Joshua.
    ▷ The golden lamp stand and the two olive trees (*Zec. 4:1-14*).
    ▷ The flying scroll (*Zec. 5:1-4*).
      * The scroll represented God's judgment upon the land. The reason for the scroll was to show the people their sins against God and each other.
    ▷ The woman in the ephah (*Zec. 5:5-11*).
      * An ephah is a basket that holds a dry measure of grain. The woman is an example of sin and rebellion. The basket is an example of God's restraining power.
    ▷ The four chariots (*Zec. 6:1-8*).
    ▷ The crowning of Joshua (*Zec. 6:9-13*).
      * Zerubabbel does this to illustrate the three-fold ministry of the coming Messiah.
        → He would build the temple.
        → He would minister as a priest.
        → He would rule as a king.
  ▶ Zechariah gave God's message to the people about their pride (*Zec. 7-8*).
    ▷ Some of the Jews asked if they could ignore the custom of fasting and mourning in the month of August.

NOTES

- ♦ God told them that because their hearts were not sincere, what they did would not matter.
  - → God told them to be honest with Him and with their neighbors.
- ▶ Zechariah gave God's message to the people about the first and second comings of the Prince (*Zec. 9-13*).
  - ▷ Zechariah prophesied several things about the first coming of Jesus Christ.
    - ♦ Jesus would feed his flock as God told him, but false shepherds would reject Him (*Zec. 11:7-8; Mat. 21:42*).
    - ♦ Jesus would make an entry of victory into Jerusalem (*Zec. 9:9; Mat. 21:1-11*).
    - ♦ Jesus would be sold for thirty pieces of silver (*Zec. 11:12; Mat. 26:15*).
    - ♦ Jesus would be crucified (*Zec. 12:10; Mat. 27:35-50*).
  - ▷ Zechariah also prophesied about the second coming of Jesus Christ.
    - ♦ Christ would appear on the Mount of Olives (*Zec. 14:4, 8*).
    - ♦ Christ will be recognized by Israel (*Zec. 12:10-14*).
    - ♦ Christ will build the temple (*Zec. 6:14*).
    - ♦ Christ will rule as Priest-King over the world (*Zec. 6:13; 9:10*).
  - ▷ Zechariah's prophecies showed that the complete restoration of Israel would happen through the coming Messiah. God had never set aside His covenant people. In fact, through Zechariah God affirmed His choice of Jerusalem (*1:16-17*). God also promised to be among His people, where He would carry out miracles to benefit them.

D. **Esther** (478-464 BC).
- King Ahasuerus of Persia replaced his queen with Esther, a young Jewish woman. Esther had kept her Jewish identity a secret for years. But when a court official planned to kill all the Jews in the land, Esther revealed her background in an effort to save her people.
  - ▶ The rise of Esther (*1-2*).
    - ▷ King Ahasuerus divorced his queen Vashti.
    - ▷ Esther, a young Jewish woman, won a beauty contest to become the new queen.
    - ▷ Esther's uncle Mordecai, a palace official, overheard and reported a plot to kill the king.
  - ▶ The lies of Haman (*3-5*).
    - ▷ A man named Haman was appointed prime minister.
    - ▷ Because Mordecai would not bow to him, Haman formed a plan to kill all the Jews in Persia.
    - ▷ Upon hearing of this plot, both Mordecai and Esther showed great courage and wisdom.
      - ♦ Mordecai's advice to Esther was to appear before King Ahasuerus and reveal her Jewish background.

- ▶ The prize of faith (*6-10*).
  - ▷ Haman was executed on the gallows he had prepared for Mordecai.
    - ◆ The king learned of Mordecai's loyalty.
    - ◆ The king learned of Haman's lies.
  - ▷ The Jews in Persia celebrated the first feast of Purim.
    - ◆ Purim would be celebrated yearly to remember the Jews' salvation from Haman.
- ▶ Esther shows that it is possible to both be loyal to an earthly government and faithful to God.
- ▶ Esther also shows that God is always at work on behalf of His people, even when His people don't recognize it.

Questions:

List a few times in your own life when God was working on your behalf, but you didn't recognize His work until much later.

What do these events tell you about God and His relationship with you? Use Scripture to support your answer.

E. **Ezra** (about 458-457 BC).
- Ezra himself led the second group of exiles back from Babylon to Jerusalem. The temple in Jerusalem had been rebuilt and dedicated around 515 BC. Ezra had the task of rebuilding the people who had rebuilt the temple.
  - ▶ The exiles had cooperation from the king (*Ezr. 7*).
    - ▷ Artaxerxes encouraged the Jews to go back to Jerusalem.
      - ◆ He wrote letters on their behalf to make their preparations and journey easier.
  - ▶ Ezra and the exiles prepared for the trip to Jerusalem (*Ezr. 8*).
    - ▷ Ezra gathered 1,500 families and 500 Levitical priests to make the journey.
    - ▷ Ezra collected around $5,000,000 from the exiles in Babylon for God's house in Jerusalem.
    - ▷ Ezra prayed and fasted for a safe trip to Jerusalem.
  - ▶ Ezra prayed for the people (*Ezr. 9*).
    - ▷ Ezra learned the people in Jerusalem had already compromised and sinned.

NOTES

- They had married pagan women and practiced pagan customs.
- Ezra confessed the sin of God's people before God.
▶ The people are purified (*Ezr. 10*).
  ▷ Many of God's people in Jerusalem were convicted of their sins. They repented and walked away from their sins.
▶ Ezra reminds us that God's people have to carefully think about how they will be different than the culture that surrounds them. Today, there are some ways in which we can take part in the culture and still honor God. Yet there are other parts of society that, as God's people, we must avoid.

Questions:

Find three ways in Ezra that God's people compromised with the culture around them. Use Scripture to support your answer.

What are some ways God's people today should not compromise with the culture around them? Discuss.

F. **Nehemiah** (445 BC).
   - Nehemiah was a close advisor to King Artaxerxes. The king released him to go to Jerusalem and build the wall of Jerusalem about 12 years after Ezra made his return to Jerusalem. Ezra and Nehemiah would work as a team to help restore God's people and their city.
     ▶ Nehemiah heard news about Jerusalem's wall (*Neh. 1*). The wall was in bad repair. It was broken down and damaged by fire.
     ▶ Nehemiah asks King Artaxerxes permission to rebuild the wall (*Neh. 2:1-8*).
       ▷ The king gave his permission. He also supplied travel documents for Nehemiah, and materials to repair the wall.
     ▶ Nehemiah inspected the wall (*Neh. 2:9-20*).
       ▷ Nehemiah returned to Jerusalem and made a night inspection of the wall.
     ▶ The people rebuilt the wall and its gates (*Neh. 3*).
     ▶ Nehemiah dealt with opposition to the wall (*Neh. 4*).
       ▷ He ignored the comments of Sanballat (the governor of Samaria), Tobiah (an Ammonite leader), and Geshem (an Arab chief).

- ♦ They often ridiculed Nehemiah and the people as they were working on the wall.
- ▷ He set guards in place to prevent attacks on the wall.
- ▷ He armed the workers with weapons as well as building tools.
- ▷ He dealt quickly with injustice and laziness among God's people (*Neh. 5*).

NOTES

Questions:

What were some of the ways Nehemiah dealt with opposition to rebuilding the wall around Jerusalem? Use Scripture to support your answer.

What are some of the ways you deal with opposition to God's work and ways? Use Scripture to support your answer.

How will you face opposition as a church planter?

- ▶ God blessed the people and the completed wall (*Neh. 6:15*).
  - ▷ God's Word was read (*Neh. 8:1-8*). The feast of tabernacles was restored (*Neh. 8:13-18*). A special covenant was made (*Neh. 9:38; 10:1-29*). Sin was denounced (*Neh. 9:1-2; 10:32-39; 13:15-22*).
- ▶ Nehemiah takes action (*Neh. 13*).
  - ▷ Nehemiah did what was needed to keep bad influences away from God's people.
- ▶ The people celebrated the completed work.
  - ▷ They ate festive meals and sent gifts to each other (*Neh. 8:12*). They sang praise songs as they walked around the wall (*Neh. 12:21-34*). The choir of Levites sang and played (*Neh. 9:4; 12:27-28*).
- ▶ Nehemiah's dedication to God was a central part of his success in restoring Jerusalem and God's people.

NOTES

G. **Malachi** (435-396 BC).
- Malachi's ministry was to warn the Jews who had returned from exile that they had neglected God. They ignored tithing. They married unbelieving wives. They did not worship from the heart. Judgment was coming, but the people who were faithful to God would find Him to be full of mercy.
  - ▶ The love of God is clear (*Mal 1:1-5*).
    - ▷ God had stated and demonstrated His love to His people. Yet His people asked, "How have you loved us?"
  - ▶ God's love is rejected (*Mal. 1:6-3:15*).
    - ▷ By the prophets:
      - ◆ They cheated the Lord through their selfish offerings (*Mal. 1:7-8*).
      - ◆ They cheated the people through their bad example (*Mal. 2:7-9*).
    - ▷ By the people:
      - ◆ Their injustice (*Mal. 2:10*).
      - ◆ Their marriages (*Mal. 2:11*).
      - ◆ Their wickedness (*Mal. 2:14*).
      - ◆ Their false worship (*Mal. 2:17*).
  - ▶ Yet God shows His love (*Mal. 3:16-4:6*).
    - ▷ By remembering His saints (*Mal. 3:16*).
    - ▷ By sending His own Son.
      - ◆ His first coming was introduced by John the Baptist (*Mal. 3:1a*).
      - ◆ His second coming will be introduced by Elijah the prophet (*Mal. 4:5*).
        - → *Malachi 3:1* tells more about what was expected of the second coming:

        "Behold, I send My messenger, and He will prepare the way before Me. And the Lord, whom you seek, will suddenly come to His temple, even the Messenger of the covenant, in whom you delight. Behold, He is coming," Says the LORD of hosts.

    - ▷ Malachi means "my messenger." *Malachi 3:1* also mentions two other messengers. The first, *"will prepare the way before Me,"* refers to John the Baptist. The second, *"the Lord... even the Messenger of the covenant,"* refers to Jesus.
    - ▷ The second coming of Jesus means the fulfillment of the covenant agreement between God and His people.
- The last words of the Old Testament are Malachi's clear anticipation of the *"great and dreadful day of the Lord."* This event was a major theme of the prophets. The emphasis of the warnings and appeals in Malachi's book are based as much on the coming judgment as on the covenant-based offer of grace. The book of Revelation gives the same expectation of judgment and repentance at the end of the New Testament (*Rev. 22:12-17*), but with greater details about the One who will return.

Questions:

What are the symptoms people have when their faith in God starts to fail? Find three places in the Return Stage where you find a symptom of failing faith. Write the symptoms and the place in the Bible where you found each one below.

1)

2)

3)

What are the signs someone has when they have faith in God? Find three places in the Return Stage where you find a sign of faith in God. Write the signs of faith and the place in the Bible where you found each one below.

1)

2)

3)

In what way will you preach and teach God's Word regarding repentance through turning to the Living Lord God?

NOTES

ENDNOTES

1. The vast majority of this book's text is adapted from Dr. H.L Willmington's *Willmington's Guide to the Bible*. Wheaton: Tyndale House Publishers, Inc. 1981.
2. Earl Radmacher, Ronald B. Allen, and H. Wayne House, eds. *Nelson's New Illustrated Bible Commentary*, (Nashville: Thomas Nelson, 1999), 14. Here the argument is made that the crucial difference was not a matter of blood sacrifice being superior, but a matter of attitude and faith in those making the sacrifices.
3. Willmington offers these insights in *Willmington's Guide to the Bible*, 12.
4. Taken from the chart "Joseph... the Foreshadow of the Savior," *Willmington's Guide to the Bible*, 58.
5. These dates are taken from *The NKJV Study Bible*, Radmacher, Allen and House, eds. (Nashville: Thomas Nelson, 2007), 91.
6. From "Israel, Enslaved in Egypt," *Willmington's Guide to the Bible*, 66.
7. *Willmington's Guide to the Bible*, 74-75.
8. *Willmington's Guide to the Bible*, 86.
9. *Willmington's Guide to the Bible*, 91.
10. Definition and explanation revised from *The NKJV Study Bible*, Earl Radmacher, Ronald Allen, and H. Wayne House, eds. (Nashville: Thomas Nelson, 2007), 408.
11. This brief and helpful history of the Ark of the Covenant follows Willmington, *Willmington's Guide to the Bible*, 109.
12. *Willmington's Guide to the Bible*, 117.
13. Revised from *Willmington's Guide to the Bible*, 126-127.
14. Revised from the chart "Synonyms for God's Revelation in Psalm 119," *The NKJV Study Bible*, 937.
15. Revised from *Willmington's Guide to the Bible*, 127-128.
16. From the chart "Proverbs: Ten Timely Themes," *Willmington's Guide to the Bible*, 134.
17. Following Donald Glenn, "Ecclesiastes," *The Bible Knowledge Commentary*, Walvoord and Zuck, eds. (Wheaton: Victor Books, 1985), 977.
18. Redacted from Henrietta Mears, *What the Bible Is All About*, p. 200, cited in *Willmington's Guide to the Bible*, 136.
19. The time periods for the writing prophets during this stage come from the chart entitled "The Writing Prophets of the Chaotic Kingdom Stage" *Willmington's Guide to the Bible*, 170.
20. *Willmington's Guide to the Bible*, 180-181.
21. *Willmington's Guide to the Bible*, "Christ in Isaiah" chart, 190.
22. Derived from *Willmington's Guide to the Bible*, 182.
23. Notes on Ezekiel 4:4-6, *The NKJV Study Bible*, Radmacher, Allen and House, eds. (Nashville: Thomas Nelson, 2007), 1262.
24. Derived from the chart "Facts on the Millennial Temple" in *Willmington's Guide to the Bible*, 224.
25. Adapted slightly from the chart "A Chronology of Christless Kings," *Willmington's Guide to the Bible*, 241.
26. *The NKJV Study Bible*, Radmacher, Allen, House, eds. (Nashville: Thomas Nelson, 2007), 755.
27. Revised from "A Chronology of the Return Stage," *Willmington's Guide to the Bible*, 245.
28. From the chart "Six Sovereign Trips," *Willmington's Guide to the Bible*, 246.
29. Willmington's Guide to the Bible, 246.

Made in the USA
Columbia, SC
26 May 2018